D0559418

STRANGE BUT TRUE
FOOTBALL STORIES

STRANGE
But True
Football
Stories

Compiled by Zander Hollander

Illustrated with Photographs

THE PUNT PASS AND KICK LIBRARY
NFL

RANDOM HOUSE
NEW YORK

Photograph credits: Vernon J. Biever, 146, 170-71; Culver
Pictures, 105; Larry Fox, 14, 16, 19; Kansas City Chiefs,
65; Ohio State University, 155; Princeton University, 38;
Susquehanna University, 51; United Press International, 4,
8-9, 23, 35, 41, 71, 81, 107, 113, 125, 129, 133, 158-59; University of Illinois, 31; Wide World, 26, 59, 88, 90, 93, 98,
140, 148, 164, 178.

This title was originally catalogued by the Library of Congress as follows:

Hollander, Zander, *comp.*
   Strange but true football stories.   New York, Random
House ₁1967₁
      viii, 184 p.   illus.   24 cm.   (The Punt, pass, and kick library)

1. Football stories.   ɪ. Title.

GV951.H58   796.332′08   67–20385

Library of Congress   ₁3₁

Trade Ed.: ISBN: 0- 394-80198-9   Lib. Ed.: ISBN: 0-394-90198-3

©Copyright, 1967, by Random House, Inc.

All rights reserved under International and Pan-American Copyright
Conventions. Published in New York by Random House, Inc., and
simultaneously in Toronto, Canada, by Random House of Canada
Limited.

Manufactured in the United States of America

Contents

Introduction

It is said that a football takes funny bounces. This refers not so much to the literally erratic path of a bouncing ball, as to the unpredictable, odd and even mysterious happenings that sometimes occur in the sport. These may involve a couple of players in need of a compass, a referee who flunks in arithmetic, an end who plays alone, a team that doesn't exist, or any number of other unlikely events.

We have culled the records of nearly a century of football drama to put together this collection of *Strange But True Football Stories*. Some of the stories started out as fragments in the memories of old timers. Others were established in football folklore. The more recent ones have ap-

peared in the sports pages. All have been tracked
down and verified—either through microfilm or
yellowed newspaper clippings or even through
actual interviews with the people involved. Nothing has been left to hearsay. No matter how
strange the stories may seem, all have been au-
thenticated.

I wish to acknowledge the contributors who
made this book possible: Maury Allen of
the New York *Post*, Joe Donnelly of *Newsday*,
Larry Fox of the New York *Daily News*, Steve
Gelman of *Life* Magazine, Phyllis Hollander of
Associated Features, Fred Katz of *Sport* Maga-
zine, Dave Sendler of *Pageant* and Jack Zanger of
Pocket Books.

Zander Hollander

STRANGE BUT TRUE
FOOTBALL STORIES

1

The Most
Surprising Tackle

Alabama fullback Tommy Lewis eagerly antici-
pated his chance to score. The Rice goal line lay
a scant 12 inches beyond the line of scrimmage
—one more foot, one more carry. An injury-rid-
dled Alabama team was threatening the heavily
favored Rice eleven in the 1954 Cotton Bowl in
Dallas, Texas. The 75,504 fans in the stadium
were hushed now, surprised by this first-quarter
Alabama drive.

Quarterback Bart Starr, an inexperienced sophomore, had been given the starting role because
of injuries to the two other quarterbacks. As
Starr leaned over and called the play in the huddle, determination tightened Lewis' face. It was
up to him to move the ball those necessary 12
inches.

Alabama came up to the line. Starr called signals, took the hand-off and planted the ball in his charging fullback's arms. Lewis saw a small hole in the Rice defense. He headed for it and charged over the goal line for the touchdown. Alabama led, 6-0. Many people in the stadium sensed an upset.

Rice's hopes for getting back into the game rested with their 6-foot, 170-pound halfback, Dicky Moegle (pronounced MAY-gull), and their

After gaining four yards, Alabama fullback Tommy Lewis is stopped by Rice halfback Dicky Moegle.

trainer Ed Wojecki. Oddly enough, the Rice trainer was almost as important as the left halfback. For Moegle, an extremely talented runner, was constantly imagining that he suffered from some ailment. Wojecki, however, was usually able to convince him that he was fit to play.

In fact, during the first quarter against Alabama, Moegle had told the trainer, "I can't make the next quarter." Wojecki reached into his bag of cure-alls and came up with a pill. The halfback gobbled it, became cheerful and announced he would continue.

Moegle may have had some unusual habits, but he also had a beautiful way of carrying a football. Alabama learned this on the first play of the second quarter. Moegle took a hand-off, cut inside the right tackle, weaved around three Alabama defenders in the secondary and raced 79 yards for a touchdown. The extra point was kicked and Rice led, 7-6.

That wiped the smiles right off the faces of Tommy Lewis and his teammates. But they weren't long in getting them back again. Alabama halfback Bill Oliver cut loose on a 54-yard run that carried Alabama deep into Rice territory. Lewis was hoping for another chance to bull his way over the goal line and regain the lead. But unfortunately for Alabama, Bart Starr had not yet become the slick quarterback who would one day lead the Green Bay Packers to so many stirring victories.

On this particular day, with the Alabama team leaning so heavily on him, Starr fumbled on the five-yard line and Rice recovered. Starr, Lewis and the rest of the offensive team left the field hoping that the defensive unit could stop Rice and Moegle.

There was little time left in the half. Rice could have run three plays and punted. With the clock running out, they would probably have gone to the locker room still holding their 7-6 advantage. But when a team has a runner like Moegle, they use him.

The front of the ball was on the five-yard line when Rice broke from their end-zone huddle and came up for the first-down play. The quarterback barked the signals for play "47F," a daring call. The F meant that the fullback was to fake a carry into the middle of the line. The 47 meant that Moegle was to get the ball and try to sweep around right end. This was a dangerous tactic for a team trapped deep in their own territory. If Alabama diagnosed the play correctly, Moegle might be driven into his own end zone. That would give Alabama a safety, adding two points to their score and giving them an 8-7 lead.

But the Rice quarterback proved to be the one who was guessing right that day. The fullback's fake deceived Alabama and then Moegle, behind good blocking, swept around his right end. He turned on his speed as he straightened his route, and headed down the right sideline. He seemed to be almost flying as he shot past the chalk lines that marked the five-yard intervals.

The huge crowd came alive to the possibility of a 95-yard touchdown run. Moegle was outdistancing his blockers as he approached the 50-yard line, and he was also running out of pursuers. Only one defensive back stood any chance at all of catching the Rice speedster. And that back would have to come from the middle of the field as Moegle sped near the Alabama bench.

Most players on the Crimson Tide's bench were watching with despair as Moegle raced by. They understood only too well that he was about to wreck Alabama's fine first-half effort. Hopelessness gripped all of them, particularly Tommy Lewis, who had contributed the most for the Crimson Tide. Then it happened.

Suddenly Lewis, number 42, leaped off the bench and cut Moegle down with a perfect tackle. Moegle tumbled to earth on the 38 and looked at Lewis in amazement. Alabama's twelfth man on the field retreated to the bench almost as quickly as he had come off it. The shocked spectators watched in disbelief.

Lewis sat down and buried his face in his

Lewis (42) comes off the bench as Moegle speeds down the sideline. A moment later, Lewis upended Moegle with a perfect tackle.

hands. Referee Cliff Shaw, going by the rules, picked up the ball and carried it the rest of the way, giving Moegle credit for a 95-yard touchdown run.

Lewis later explained sheepishly: "I guess I'm too full of Alabama. He just ran too close. I didn't know what I was doing. After I pulled him down, I jumped up and got back on the bench and kept telling myself: 'I didn't do it. I didn't do it.' But I knew I did."

Realizing that Lewis' intense pride in Alabama had led to his spontaneous tackle, the officials permitted the fullback to remain in the game. Alabama needed every available healthy player if they were to keep up with Moegle.

But Lewis' presence wasn't enough. Moegle scored a third touchdown as Rice went on to a 28-6 victory. Moegle had gained 265 yards in 11 carries—an average of 24.1 yards per carry—and he won the game's Most Valuable Player award.

Because of one impetuous tackle, Tommy Lewis and Dickey Moegle were to be forever linked in football history.

Dick Moegle eventually became the manager of a motel in Houston, Texas. In an interview he told sports writers that he and Lewis often wrote to each other.

"Tommy's in the insurance business now in Alabama," Moegle revealed. "But after graduation he was coaching a high school team. He got his team into a play-off for the state championship.

"They were leading, 12-7, with about a minute to go. A back on the other team got loose. While he was running, one of Lewis' kids jumped off the bench and tackled the runner. The officials gave the team a touchdown and Tommy's team lost, 13-12. I don't think he'd been teaching that sort of thing, but it sure must have rubbed off."

Had the high school lad's tackle been prompted by his knowledge of his coach's famous bench tackle, or was it just a case of football history repeating itself?

2

When Disaster Struck Cumberland

In 1916, a world war was raging in Europe, but most Americans were confident that President Woodrow Wilson would continue to keep the United States out of the fighting. Football fans were still more interested in thinking about their favorite sport, especially at Georgia Tech where the Engineers were putting together the beginnings of a powerful football team.

That spring, as the school was completing its fall schedule, a letter was sent to little Cumberland College in Lebanon, Tennessee. The letter was addressed to the "football manager" and it asked if the Bulldogs would be interested in playing Tech in Atlanta on October 7 for a $500 guarantee.

Cumberland had once been a football power-house. The Bulldogs had been undefeated from 1903 through 1905, and during this time they had claimed the Southern championship. Ten years later the school still fielded an organized football team of sorts and some of Cumberland's old reputation still remained. Georgia Tech thought that a victory over the Bulldogs would be good for the Engineers' prestige.

College football at the time of World War I was not restrained by any of the tight rules that now limit the sport. Almost anybody connected with a school could play, and "ringers" often were brought in under assumed names. Graduate students usually made up the schedules (seeking the best deals they could), organized the team and acted as coaches. Sometimes these "coaches" also played. John Heisman at Tech, in fact, was the school's first full-time coach.

The situation was still informal at Cumberland, where there wasn't even a football manager. As a result, the letter from Georgia Tech found its way into the hands of a senior named M. S. McGregor. McGregor had played football at Cumberland and was manager of the baseball team. Though he was going to be graduated in June, he was helping the school put together a football schedule for the following fall. He read the letter, saw the offer of a $500 guarantee and quickly accepted the invitation for Cumberland.

This was McGregor's final connection with what was to become a historic game. He took his degree that spring and entered the teaching profession.

By the next fall, Cumberland had a football manager named George Allen. He had been on the 1915 team and had been promoted to executive duties. His job was to see that Cumberland showed up at Tech and to collect the $500 after the game. (Allen later became director of the federal government's Reconstruction Finance Corporation and an advisor to several United States Presidents.)

The week of the big game approached and the outlook was not bright for little Cumberland, for the Bulldogs had lost several key players as a result of injuries in previous games. Allen, however, was not dismayed.

First, he scoured the campus for recruits and came up with a husky farm boy from rural Texas named Gentry Dugat. Dugat had played only two games of football in his life, one in high school and the other in prep school. He didn't even know what a down was. He joined the team because Allen promised him his first Pullman-car ride, as well as a chance to visit the birthplace of his idol, Henry Grady, a great Atlanta newspaper editor.

Gentry Dugat, who didn't even know the meaning of a "down" in football.

But Allen had another, more important ace to play before putting his outmanned team on the field against Georgia Tech. The train which the Cumberland players took to Atlanta would make a long stopover in Nashville, Tennessee, where Vanderbilt University is located. Vanderbilt had a good football team and Allen was certain he could recruit some of their players for his team.

That stop in Nashville was the turning point on a journey that sent the Cumberland players on to immortality. As the train chugged to a halt, Allen leaped off and headed for the Vanderbilt campus. He had dreams of returning with many muscled athletes in tow, but he was cruelly disappointed. Vanderbilt had a big game coming up and couldn't spare a man. To make matters worse, three Cumberland players got lost in Nashville and missed the train. The only recruit Allen could find was a Nashville newspaperman named Jack Nelson. Nelson had once attended Cumberland, and he played in the game that day under a false name. Only 16 players, including Dugat, Nelson and two or three injured regulars, finally got to Atlanta.

And what a team they faced! The Tech Yellow Jackets would achieve an 8-0-1 record in 1916, and begin a 33-game winning streak. Eight of the players who performed against Cumberland would make All-Southern at least once before graduating, and two of the tackles would make All-America. The following season Tech would win nine games in a row and claim the national football title. Coach Heisman would eventually be chosen for college football's Hall of Fame, and so would his assistant, Bill Alexander.

Cumberland's coach was a law student from Dallas named Butch McQueen, who graduated at mid-term that year and never appeared again in the sports world.

The game started as a rout and degenerated from there. Tech used 30 players in the game against only 14 for Cumberland. The Atlanta team scored a record 63 points in the first period, equaled that total in the second, then added 54 more in the third and 42 in the fourth quarter. Cumberland was never even close to a touchdown. The final score—222-0! It was the most one-sided college football game ever played.

The teams were supposed to play four quar-

Dow R. Cope played left tackle for Cumberland.

ters, each 12½ minutes long, but they quickly
decided to play two quarters of 12 minutes and
two of 10 minutes. After the half, however, with
Tech leading, 126-0, the remaining quarters were
cut to 10 and 7½ minutes, respectively. To the
battered and beaten Bulldogs, though, the short-
ened game time still seemed endless.

Cumberland's only encouragement came from
manager Allen, who ran up and down the sidelines yelling, "Hang in there. We need the $500."
Later he spent most of the profits showing his
players the sights of Atlanta.

Among the records set were: most points in one
game (breaking Michigan's mark of 153 in 1912);
most yards gained (978); most players scoring
touchdowns (13); most points kicked after touchdown by one player (18 straight by Jim Preas in
the first half); and most points in one quarter
(63, twice). Everett Strupper, Tech's left halfback, scored seven touchdowns himself and was
heading for an eighth, late in the game, when
he suddenly downed the ball on Cumberland's
one-yard line.

Canty Alexander, Tech's huge and likable
right guard, had never scored a touchdown in
his college career. His teammates decided to let
him get one. Alexander was grateful, but cautious.
During the preceding game, his buddies also had
promised him an easy touchdown and then re-

fused to block for him. They had howled with laughter as he was snowed under on three straight plays. This time Alexander made his teammates swear they would block, and as the ball was snapped he watched to make sure they did. He concentrated so hard on his teammates that the ball bounced off his chest. He still had time to pick the ball up, however. As he recalled years later, "I pranced across like a debutante."

Skimpy game records credit Cumberland fullback A. L. McDonald with completing a 10-yard pass for the Bulldogs' longest gain. But McDonald insisted that this was an error. "I made our longest gain of the day when I lost five yards around right end," he said.

At a reunion of players from both sides 40 years later, right halfback Morris Gouger disputed both the record and his teammate. "In one of the smartest bits of football strategy on record, in the closing minutes of the game with fourth down and 25 to go, deep in our own territory, I called for a quarterback sneak. That play saved us from a really ignominious defeat. If we had punted as we should have, Tech would have blocked the kick and scored again."

At another point in the game, Cumberland was fielding one of Tech's many kickoffs and the safetyman fumbled the ball. As the ball spun away toward a teammate, the fumbler yelled,

Charles E. Edwards, Cumberland's quarterback, was so ashamed of his role in the mismatch that he refused to attend the team's 40-year reunion.

"Hey, pick it up." The teammate saw the onrushing horde of tacklers and replied, "You pick it up, you dropped it."

Years later Cumberland grads denied the story. "We may have been badly beaten and unskilled, but we were not yellow," Dugat said.

"My heart felt for them at the time," said Froggy Morrison, a member of the Tech squad who didn't get into the game. "They were limited in size and number of substitutes, but they bore their burden inside and took it."

Canty Alexander added, "It takes a lot of guts to fight on with all hope out of sight."

This is something that Cumberland quarterback Charles Edwards should have kept in mind. Forty years later he was still so ashamed of his part in football's greatest mismatch that he refused to answer any letters inviting him to the reunion.

3

Upstarts from the Other League

The bitterness between the Cleveland Browns and the Philadelphia Eagles had been building for years and finally, on September 17, 1950, it was about to explode in a showdown. In all the decades of professional football, an opening-day game had never before attracted so much interest. The reason was that the first game of the 1950 season would, in effect, determine the championship of the 1949 season.

In 1949 the Eagles had won the National Football League title and the Browns had won the All-America Football Conference title. But the two leagues had been at war in 1949, so the important issue of which team was the true champion of pro football had not been settled.

When the AAFC was first organized, in 1946, NFL fans immediately began to minimize the talent of AAFC teams. Some people would admit that the rival league had a few genuine stars, but they contended that the AAFC couldn't be compared team for team with the NFL. These people would cite the NFL's age and experience as the bases for their arguments. George Marshall, the former laundry tycoon who owned the NFL's Washington Redskins, said, "Our weakest team could toy with their best."

Then in January, 1950, the two leagues had merged, giving the Browns a chance to prove that they could beat not only the weakest NFL team, but also the best. The Browns knew that Greasy Neale, the Eagles' coach, had said, "Cleveland's just a basketball team. All they can do is throw." And they knew that another of the NFL's old guard had called them "a podunk team with a high-school coach."

The bitterness existing between the two leagues was clearly evident at a banquet that took place only a few months before the beginning of the 1950 season. Otto Graham, the Cleveland quarterback, was on the speaker's platform and at one point he said, "Maybe Mr. Marshall better buy back a piece of his old laundry business if we play the Redskins next year."

Hearing this, Marshall leaped up and shouted,

Coach Paul Brown with quarterback Otto Graham during a practice session.

"You probably won't even have a job next year. Maybe you'd like to *drive* one of those laundry trucks."

So, as the showdown neared, the Browns were proud, angry and determined. But they still were not expected to win. Football experts pointed out that the Eagles had pride, determination and talent, too. And, most important of all, they had the experience of playing together for years in the oldest and biggest professional football league in the country.

The Eagles had tough linemen—Pete Pihos, Bucko Kilroy, Norm Wiley, Al Wistert, Chuck Bednarik and Alex Wojciechowicz, the old Fordham "block of granite." They had a slick quarterback, Tommy Thompson, who had proven himself under NFL championship pressure. They also had the best running back in pro football— Steve Van Buren. Although he had been injured and would not play in the all-important game, his position had been adequately filled by the proven pro star and college All-America, Clyde "Smackover" Scott.

The Browns had a smart coach, Paul Brown, and many experienced players: quarterback Graham, ends Mac Speedie and Dante Lavelli, linemen Bill Willis, Abe Gibron, Lou Groza and Frank Gatski, and the bulldozing fullback, 238-pound Marion Motley. These men had earned their reputations in the AAFC, helping to win four consecutive championships in what many experts called "a minor league." In 1950 they had to prove they could star in the big leagues, too.

There were 71,237 people in Philadelphia's Municipal Stadium as the game began. The Eagles received the kickoff, but they couldn't gain ground and punted. On the Cleveland 20-yard line, rookie safetyman Don Phelps watched the ball spiral toward him. He caught it and sped 80 yards into the end zone, but a clipping penalty against Cleveland nullified the touchdown.

Up in the stands Eagle fans were saying that the 80-yard run was merely a fluke. The Browns would not have a chance to score in the hard, solid football that would be played from scrimmage for four quarters.

The Eagles stopped the Browns, then took command of the football and drove to the Cleveland 15. From there, with roughly half of the first period over, Cliff Patton kicked a Philadelphia field goal.

The Browns blazed back. From scrimmage, Otto Graham faded to his 41 and floated a pass to halfback Dub Jones. Snaking free, Jones caught the ball on the Eagle 25 and ran for a touchdown. Forrest Grigg kicked the extra point and the upstarts were ahead, 7-3.

In the second quarter, Paul Brown, sending in plays from the sidelines, called for a hook-pass to end Mac Speedie. Following instructions, Graham dropped into his protective pocket behind Motley, snapped back his arm and prepared to throw. But suddenly he saw his other end, Lavelli, far behind the Eagle defense and in the clear. Graham readjusted his aim and threw. Lavelli caught the pass and the Browns had another touchdown.

At the half Cleveland led, 14-3. In the stands people weren't saying "minor leaguers" very often. Not only was Graham penetrating the Eagles with his short, snappy sideline passes and his long, floating bombs, but the Cleveland defense was even managing to stifle the Eagle offensive drive. Although Motley had fumbled on his own five-yard line in the second quarter and the Eagles had recovered, they had moved nowhere. They had tried four running plays, and Motley, who played linebacker on goal-line stands, had made three of the four tackles.

In the third quarter Graham threw a 13-yard

Left end Mac Speedie takes a pass from Graham for a 19-yard gain.

touchdown pass to Speedie. But early in the fourth quarter the Eagles scored on a 17-yard pass from Bill Mackrides to Pihos. The score was 21-10 after the Eagle extra point. Again the Philadelphia fans glowed with confidence. They felt that there was still plenty of time for two touchdowns and a victory.

Indeed, two more touchdowns were scored, but by the Browns. And they didn't score them by passing. In the fourth quarter the Brown runners began to bore through the five-man Eagle line and past the two linebackers. On play after play, Motley, Jones and halfback Rex Bumgardner swept into the secondary. Bumgardner scored one of the touchdowns on a two-yard run; Graham scored the other on a one-yard sweep.

The Browns won, 35-10, and anyone with sense had to admit that, even if Steve Van Buren had played, the Eagles would still have been beaten. As strange as it might seem, the upstarts from the new league really were pro football's best.

4

Just for Kicks

His parents had named him Forrest, but everybody called him "Frosty"—Frosty Peters. He loved the freedom of the outdoors in his native Montana and he was the sort of natural athlete who excelled at everything he tried. Whether he was hurling the javelin or kicking a football, socking a baseball or driving a golf ball, Frosty made it look as easy as strolling down the street.

As a freshman at Montana State University, however, he was best known for his skills on the football field. Playing quarterback on the freshman team, he was especially gifted as a dropkicker. Straight through the 1924 season, the Bobkittens, as the Montana freshmen were called, had remained unbeaten. As a result, their spirits were high when they took the field against Billings Polytechnic on a Saturday in November.

On the very first play from scrimmage, Frosty took the ball, broke through the Poly defense and ran free and clear downfield. A few yards away from a touchdown, he suddenly stopped, turned around as if he had remembered something and then scampered back to the Poly 10-yard line. There he promptly dropped the ball and drop-kicked it squarely between the goal posts for a field goal.

Puzzled Bobkitten rooters didn't know whether to cheer or to boo at this odd behavior. Where Montana State should have had six points they now had only three. But Frosty's coach, Schubert Dyche, and his teammates were obviously not upset. It seemed as if they knew that something like this was going to happen.

After Montana State kicked off, they held the Poly offense and regained control of the ball. Then the Bobkitten captain, Big Jim Ario, took a long pass from Frosty and headed into open territory. Big Jim wanted a touchdown badly, because he hadn't scored one all season and this was his chance. But, as if by plan, he stopped churning when he reached the Poly 15-yard line. He ended the play right there by putting the ball on the ground. On the next play Frosty Peters drop-kicked his second field goal.

This unusual pattern marked the rest of the

first half as Frosty's fellow players insisted on giving up their own scoring opportunities in favor of their drop-kicking quarterback. By the time the first half ended, Frosty had drop-kicked nine field goals in 14 attempts.

During the intermission at halftime, Frosty pleaded with his teammates, "I've had my share. When you fellows have a chance to score, take it." But the entire Bobkitten squad, backed by coach Dyche, voted him down. They had their reasons.

The second half went much as the first. Each time the Montana State frosh got within range, they would halt the action and give Frosty another drop kick. By the time Frosty was taken out of the game in the fourth period, with 10 minutes remaining, he had had 22 chances at field goals and he had made good 17 of them! His valuable right foot had accounted for 51 points.

It was only then that the Bobkittens added a couple of touchdowns to make the final score: Montana State 64, Billings Poly 0.

Afterward the Bobkitten coach revealed why the team had set up Frosty with his field goals. "We wanted a world record for Frosty and we got it," said Dyche.

Until then, nobody in high school, college or professional football had ever kicked more than 15 field goals in one game. (An Exeter, Califor-

Frosty Peters

nia, high-school lad named Griggs had booted 15 in 1915, and a Purdue collegian named Robertson had set the college mark in 1900 with a total of seven field goals.) Coach Dyche not only wanted to secure the record for his prize kicker; he also wanted to show that his freshmen had the spirit, cooperation and ability to achieve such a remarkable feat.

Ironically, Frosty's 17 field goals drew the attention of Bob Zuppke, the famous coach of the

University of Illinois. "We want you at Illinois," Zuppke told Peters after the 1924 season. So Frosty never played again at Montana State. Instead, he transferred to Illinois. He became a star there, too, but, curiously, his passing stood out even more than his kicking. In one victory over Ohio State, he completed nine aerials in a row.

After college, Frosty played some professional football and for a while he served as a minor league baseball umpire. But nothing else he ever did matched the incredible total of 17 field goals he scored in that one game played while he was a fuzzy-cheeked freshman at Montana State.

The record still stands after more than 40 years.

5

Twelfth Man

On the morning of November 23, 1935, football fans along the Eastern Seaboard were dismayed when they looked out of their windows. The day for the showdown between undefeated Dartmouth and undefeated Princeton had finally arrived, and snow was falling without letup!

Already, excitement over the game had risen to such a pitch that unscrupulous people outside Princeton's Palmer Stadium were able to sell tickets for as much as $50 apiece. Dartmouth, swift and precise, had beaten such formidable teams as Harvard, Yale, Cornell and Brown. Princeton had lost just one game in three years—7-0 to Yale in 1934—and had the advantage of playing on its home field.

Dartmouth and Princeton fans were so excited by the match that even the forbidding weather couldn't keep them at home. While they were wrapping themselves in layers of clothing and setting out early for the stadium, the Dartmouth team was already there, fretting in the dressing room.

The Indian squad wasn't afraid of Princeton. Rather, the problem was one of equipment; Dartmouth had forgotten to bring along mud cleats. Coach Earl Blaik looked forlornly out the window of the fieldhouse and watched the wet snow turn the playing surface into treacherous mush. The muddy field was made to order for the Tigers' straight-ahead power, but it would be disastrous for the Dartmouth team, which depended on quick cuts and reverses.

Then came a knock on the door. It was Fritz Crisler, Princeton coach. "Say," he said. "I hear your boys don't have mud cleats. We're using them, and you can borrow some of ours."

Blaik just shook his head. "Thanks," he replied, "but it just won't work." The Dartmouth players wore a special kind of football shoe, which couldn't be adapted for the standard mud cleat. So the team went out for pre-game drills wearing normal-length cleats. In the words of one Dartmouth player, "It was like playing on grease."

Though the snowfall hadn't abated by game time, a noisy crowd of 56,000 packed the stadium, waiting tensely for the action. It came swiftly and surprisingly. The aggressive Dartmouth team, using a single-wing formation, built early momentum despite the lack of mud cleats. Then, with a quick burst, Indian wingback Pop Nairne took the ball on a Statue of Liberty play, moved around right end, and went 24 yards to the Princeton one-yard line. Fullback John Handrahan charged over for the score. Although Dartmouth missed the extra point, nothing but joyous shouts came from the visitors' side of the field.

Already, however, the game had taken on an eerie quality. Watching it through the snow was like peering at moving silhouettes through a transparent white curtain. The lines on the field were covered, and the officials had to dig for them each time a measurement was required.

After Dartmouth's score, Princeton began to assert itself. The Tigers found Dartmouth's weak spot—the middle of the line—and shifty little Paul Pauk squirted through a hole on the left side and went 33 yards for a touchdown. Ken Sandback's place kick put Princeton ahead, 7-6.

As the afternoon wore on, Princeton picked up more momentum and the cheering from the home side of the stadium grew louder. The Tigers' offense drove 48 yards for another score so that

Dartmouth kicker punts successfully while players scramble on the mushy field in the 1935 Princeton game.

Princeton led, 13-6, at the half. Then, after a third-quarter Dartmouth drive foundered on Princeton's 21-yard line, the Tigers again exploited the Dartmouth middle, scoring a third touchdown. Gamely the Indian captain and linebacker, Jack Kenney, continued challenging the Tigers. "Come on," he kept yelling, "try to shoot one through here."

The snow had turned to sleet, but none of the fans had left. Late in the fourth quarter, Princeton's offense pushed the Indians back on their own six-yard line, where the Indians made their stand. Princeton punched straight ahead, but netted just three yards in two plays. Then, as the Tigers wheeled from their huddle for the third-down play, they saw an incredible sight.

Splashing across the end zone onto the playing field came a spectator who seemed determined to enter the game. He stumbled into place on the Dartmouth line between tackle Dave Camerer and guard Joe Handrahan. "Kill those Princeton guys," he bellowed. Then, before the players could recover from their surprise, he leaped across the line at the nearest Princeton man—and fell flat on his face.

"The whole Princeton line," recalls Camerer, "manhandled the poor guy unmercifully until the cops collared him and dragged him off, his heels cutting a double track in the snow. I was truly sorry to see him leave."

After being manhandled by Princeton's linemen, the "Twelfth Man" in the Dartmouth line is dragged off the field by policemen.

Jack White ran up the middle for the last Princeton touchdown and, in the confusion following the 26-6 victory, no one could find the man who had tried to save the day for Dartmouth.

He had made history as Dartmouth's famed "Twelfth Man." But as Stanley Woodward noted in the New York *Herald Tribune*, he "was an orphan without intercollegiate affiliations, mother, father, country or home." Woodward added that he had "great admiration for any man so courageous as to willfully place himself in the way of that Princeton team. As I see it, he deserves more than the unclaimed notoriety he is getting and the solid kick in the trousers he got from Weller of Princeton."

Soon after, two men stepped forward to take the credit. But their claims could not be substantiated, and the matter was never settled.

In a year-end poll, the Associated Press sports writers voted the incident the number-one oddity of 1935. And whoever the "Twelfth Man" was, Dartmouth will be forever grateful. As Camerer pointed out, "The way Princeton was ripping through us, we needed all the help we could get."

6

The Littlest
Pass-Master

Even in his padded suit and helmet he didn't look very big, standing among the giants who surrounded him in the Philadelphia Eagles' huddle. But little Davey O'Brien, all 5 feet 7 inches of him, was a brilliant and resourceful field general, who knew that it took more than size to be a winner. Even more, he was a gifted and daring passer. On this day of December 1, 1940 he was playing his farewell game in professional football, and he wanted to leave something behind for people to talk about after he had gone. He did.

This was O'Brien's second year with the Eagles. It was also his final year and he was playing his farewell game in professional football. Before the game, he had announced that he was retiring to work for the FBI.

O'Brien was concluding a remarkable foot-

Little Davey O'Brien of Texas Christian passes against Arkansas.

ball career that had begun at Texas Christian University. There, he broke almost every Southwest Conference passing record and led the Horned Frogs to two national titles in a row. In his senior year he won both the Heisman and Maxwell awards as the outstanding collegiate football player of 1938.

But despite his feats, he didn't think he would succeed in pro football. He was too small, everybody said. Even Davey had to agree, and at first he was reluctant to sign a pro contract. But the Eagles managed to change his mind. In his rookie year, he was the NFL's second-leading passer, was named to the all-league team, and established three new passing marks, including 21 completions in one game.

As a result, O'Brien was well known to football fans when he came on the field to direct the hapless Eagles against the might of the Washington Redskins. The Eagles had won only one game all season and were mired in last place. The Redskins were seeking the victory that would assure them of first place in the Eastern Division of the NFL. Many fans regarded the game as the mismatch of the year.

A capacity crowd of 25,833 had jammed Washington's Griffith Stadium by kickoff time. Despite the uneven match, neither side could score in the first quarter. The Eagle line was outweighed and outrushed by the Redskin forwards, who threw back the Eagle runners for more yards than they could gain. So, early in the second period, little Davey took to the air. He began to fill the air with more passes than any pro-football crowd had ever seen before. Not even the dynamic Redskins seemed capable of stopping him. The Redskins did manage to break through on the scoreboard, however, on a 27-yard reverse by wingback Wilbur Moore. The Redskins missed the extra point and led, 6-0.

But O'Brien did not relax his passing attack. To elude the onrushing tacklers, he faded back as far as 15 and 20 yards behind the line of scrimmage, picked out his receivers and completed his passes. And when he couldn't find anyone free, he ran with the ball. On two successive plays he gained 34 yards on runs, nearly twice as many as the rest of the team would make on the ground all day. He mounted a drive that carried the Eagles 64 yards in five plays, and seemed headed for the tying touchdown when the halftime gun went off. In all, Davey had completed 11 passes for 112 yards in the first half.

That was only a warmup for what was to come. He continued his assault in the second half. Despite the growing pressure being put on him by the Redskin linemen, Davey managed to connect on passes with ridiculous ease. He passed wide to the side and he passed deep; he threw from behind his own goal line and he threw on the dead run, riddling the Redskin defense with his slingshot passes.

He was little David against the Goliaths of the league, a sprite standing up against the six-foot, 230-pounders who seemed to be trying to separate his head from his shoulders. Often enough they got to him and smashed the little man to the ground. But each time he would pick himself off the turf and go back to work. Every now and then a Redskin lineman would help him to his feet, apologizing for having knocked him down.

Meanwhile, the Redskins, masterminded by Sammy Baugh, who had preceded O'Brien at TCU, scored on Dick Todd's plunge from the four-yard line. With Bob Masterson's kick the Redskins now led, 13-0. Still, O'Brien would not quit. Playing all the way on offense and defense, he stimulated another Eagle drive. He engineered two drives in the third period, one of them for 68 yards in 12 plays, and another for 66 yards in five plays. But the Eagles still couldn't get the ball across the Redskin goal line.

The Eagles' predicament looked even gloomier in the fourth quarter when Baugh, an excellent punter, quick-kicked, and the ball traveled 85 yards before it was downed on the three-yard line. But O'Brien charged up the Eagles once more. He began pumping passes immediately. His primary target was left end Don Looney, who was to catch a record 14 passes for 180 yards during the day. In 15 plays, he drove the Eagles all the way, finally scoring with a 13-yard pass to fullback Frank Emmons. The try for the extra point was blocked, and the Eagles trailed, 13-6.

Time was running out now, but not O'Brien's courage. As soon as the Eagles got the ball again, O'Brien began one last drive that carried them down to the Redskins' 33-yard line. He was still flinging passes into the end zone, trying for the tying score while being rushed by six or seven men at once. But with 17 seconds showing on the clock, and O'Brien's endurance waning, Coach Bert Bell took him out of the game. He had played for 59 minutes and 43 seconds of a grueling football game, and he had thrown an unprecedented total of 60 passes. And not one of them was intercepted! Overall, Davey completed 33 of his passes for 316 yards.

As Davey came to the sidelines, a dejected little figure in a mud-caked jersey with the numeral 5 on it, everyone in the ballpark stood up and cheered for his remarkable demonstration of courage and skill. Even the Redskin players openly applauded him as he walked off the football field for the last time. The Eagles were beaten, 13-6, but not vanquished.

Davey's performance that day remains an indelible memory, even though most of his marks have since been erased. But the one that still stands is his 60 passes.

Although the Eagles had lost, the fans in Griffith Stadium could not complain of a dull game. They had witnessed a thrilling near-upset and a performance by a diminutive quarterback that has become part of football history.

O'Brien's teammates congratulate him after his gallant but futile effort against the Redskins. He completed 33 of a record 60 passes.

7

College President on the Bench

When Dr. Gustave Weber put the phone back on its cradle on that October Sunday in 1965, he was momentarily stunned. He was a college president without a football coach. And there were two more games to go on the Susquehanna University football schedule.

No amount of persuasion by Dr. Weber could convince Jim Garrett to stay. Garrett was a proud, intense man. Through five seasons he had carved out an outstanding winning record at Susquehanna—39 victories, four losses and one tie. But the 1965 season had been a disaster for a man who was used to winning. Susquehanna had lost all seven of the games it had played so far.

Every coach with a record of success is entitled to a lean year, even a season of straight defeats, and certainly Garrett could have remained at Susquehanna. But he was a perfectionist who took football seriously, perhaps too seriously. While his teams were still winning, he had posted a sign at the field which read: "Through these portals pass the world's best football players." After two 1965 losses, he had taken it down.

His action didn't help his team's morale very much. Five straight losses followed. That was when Garrett called Dr. Weber to say that the players were no longer responding to him. He was leaving and so were his assistant coaches.

After Weber was convinced that he couldn't change Garrett's mind, he had a sudden inspiration. The next day he announced his decision. Susquehanna's football coach for the remaining two games of the season would be Dr. Gustave Weber.

His decision put an instant spotlight on Selinsgrove, Pennsylvania, where Susquehanna is located. Reporters from all over the nation called and wanted to know how the college president, who was also a Lutheran minister, could hope to coach a football team.

"I couldn't have received more publicity if I'd robbed a bank," Dr. Weber said. "A reporter called me from a New York newspaper and asked if I was going to change my formation. He must have thought I didn't know anything about football. I told him, 'Well, the rules won't allow us to use the guards back or the flying wedge.' "

Actually the 57-year-old educator had more experience than most realized. In the late 1920s he had been a nine-letter man at Wagner College in Staten Island, New York—playing football, baseball and basketball. Still, his only football coaching experience had been at the junior varsity high school level. This was not really solid preparation for the college game.

As soon as Dr. Weber could get rid of the reporters and their questions, he went to meet with his team. The first thing he told his players was that football is only a game. He suspected that they hadn't had much fun playing it so far that season, but he hoped the situation would change during the final two games. He also added a pass play to their strategy. Garrett had been a great believer in keeping the football near the ground. This method can lead to an efficient offense, but almost always produces a dreary game. All in all, Dr. Weber made quite an impression on his team.

"This might lead to a real fad, with all of the college presidents all over the country taking over as coaches," said Bill Gagne, a Susquehanna team captain. Probably the only people not rooting for Dr. Weber, aside from Susquehanna's next two opponents, were college football coaches.

As the game with Geneva drew near, Dr. Weber appointed his coaching assistants—an alumni director and a faculty member. When someone asked Dr. Weber what it is like to take over a team that has lost seven games in a row, he answered: "My philosophy is that if someone gives you a lemon, make lemonade."

Susquehanna opened against Geneva with a surprise play—a completed pass. "I told them to open with a long pass," Coach Weber later admitted. "I've been trying to tell Garrett to do it for six years, but he always opened the game with an off-tackle play. He did it so much, he might as well have announced it. We faked off-tackle and threw."

Before Geneva could do anything about it, Susquehanna was leading, 6-0. That first touchdown provided a great moment at Selinsgrove. In the seven previous games Susquehanna had scored only 27 points, in contrast to 191 scored by their opponents. Now Susquehanna was leading early in the game.

Fans acclaimed Dr. Gustave Weber as a coaching genius and announced their opinion with a sign that said, "Gus-Au-Go-Go." Coach Weber signaled his quarterback to pass for the two-point conversion try. It missed, but the fans yelled support for his daring.

During the game there were several occasions

Dr. Weber gives instructions to his players during Susquehanna's meeting with Geneva College.

when many coaches would have questioned Dr.
Weber's strategy. After Geneva took a 7-6 lead,
Susquehanna had the ball fourth-and-two on its
own 37. In a situation like this, most coaches
would punt, but not Dr. Weber. He ordered a run
and it was successful—first down! Then it was
fourth down and four yards to go near midfield.
Dr. Weber sent in his punter, but the punter
passed—the surprise play Coach Weber had in-
stalled. Soon Susquehanna led, 14-7.

Dr. Weber's team kept the pressure on and

held a 22-21 lead at half time. The lead slipped away, however, in the last quarter. Geneva drew ahead, 29-22. But Susquehanna stayed in the battle right to the end. With two minutes and 30 seconds to play, they scored, trailing by only a point, 29-28.

This presented an opportunity to play for a tie or a win. Susquehanna could try the safer route of kicking for one point, or go all out for two points on a run or a pass. Dr. Weber hadn't wavered all afternoon and he didn't now. Susquehanna went for the win on a run, but the play was stopped and the game was over.

It had been an exciting afternoon, a fun-filled afternoon. Susquehanna had now lost eight games in a row, but the team had scored more points in just one Saturday than in the previous seven.

The team also lost to Tufts University the following Saturday, 41-28. Coach Weber returned to being just plain Dr. Gustave Weber, college president. He had few regrets about his two games as coach, although he did say, "If I had known that I would receive so much publicity, I wouldn't have taken the job. I could do something really important in the field of education—and nobody would pay any attention."

But the nation had paid attention because people admired the spirit and courage of a college president who didn't let his school down.

8

99 plus 1

The Yale varsity was running through signal drills on the Friday morning before the 1952 Harvard game. In the middle of the workout, Coach Jordan Olivar grinned broadly and blew his whistle. "Okay fellas," Olivar commanded, "let's run Charlie's play." The players chuckled and someone yelled for Charlie Yeager.

Team manager Charlie Yeager, five-foot six-inch, 140-pound senior, dropped the bag of footballs he was checking and hurried out toward the center of the field. Usually, when a player called for Charlie, he needed some tape, a new lace for his shoes, or some minor first aid. But this time it was different. Olivar, a shrewd judge of men, was running the play both to encourage Charlie and to relax his players for Saturday's struggle with Harvard.

The coach knew how Yeager loved football and recognized how thrilled he would be to run a play with the varsity. So Olivar had devised an extra-point play that Yale would save for the right occasion; that is, when the score was high enough to risk the play. They would use Charlie's play after scoring a touchdown, when Yale would normally kick for the extra point. But instead of doing the expected, Yale would fake the place kick in favor of a pass to Yeager, who would try to run the ball into the end zone.

Forgetting Harvard momentarily, the players laughed easily as they watched Charlie scramble out for the pass. And the earnest little manager, though smiling, ran his pass pattern with care. He was hoping for the miracle that would permit him to score for the Yale varsity.

The Elis, with a 6-2 record going into this last game of the season, bristled with anticipation. They knew that a victory would result in Yale's most successful football season since 1946. Besides, they were playing their traditional rivals. The current Bulldogs knew the legend of the Yale coach who once told his players, "Gentlemen, you are about to meet Harvard in a game of football. Never again in your lives will you do anything as important."

The Harvard team, always formidable at home, was just as eager to meet Yale. So far they had a record of five won and three lost in the 1952 season and were spoiling for the chance to stage an upset. The game would match the Crimson's triple-threat tailback, Dick Clasby, against Yale's gifted passer, Ed Molloy. All week long, sports writers and fans had been debating the outcome, and ticket sales were moving briskly.

As Charlie Yeager assembled the team's gear, for the Friday afternoon trip to Boston, he made certain that he packed a uniform for himself— just in case. The only jersey small enough to fit him was number 99.

Between noon on Friday and the kickoff at 1:30 P.M. on Saturday, the team manager had much to accomplish. First, Charlie and his staff of 12 underclassmen put the team and its equipment on the train at the New Haven station. Then they herded men and baggage to the hotel in Boston, and gave the hotel staff instructions about what to serve the players for Friday dinner and Saturday breakfast. On Saturday morning Charlie made provisions for the boys to have their ankles taped at the hotel. Then he made sure they were on the buses for Harvard Stadium by noon.

It was not an ideal day for football. Raw winds bucked erratically across the floor of the stadium and whipped vigorously against the faces of the 37,114 people filling the stands. The ground itself was ominously moist. But, as the Bulldogs rushed through the stadium tunnel to get to the field, Charlie realized that the excited squad scarcely noticed the inclement weather.

No one could have known it at the time, but the game program contained an ironic hint of what would be the day's most unusual play. The artist's drawing on the cover showed several Yale men—one wearing number 99—sweeping up the field.

Yale started off the game with an air of invincibility. The Elis powered 55 yards to a touchdown the second time they had possession of the ball. They scored when fullback Jimmy Jones went 38 yards up the middle without being touched by a Harvard player.

Although Dick Clasby and fullback John Culver then led Harvard down to the Yale 13-yard line, the Elis threw up just enough resistance to hold them. First, an offside penalty nullified a Crimson first down and then Yale trapped Clasby for a 20-yard loss on an attempted pass.

Early in the second quarter, Yale moved in to score after linebacker Joe Fortunato intercepted a pass on the Harvard 39. They made the touchdown on a short pass from Molloy to end Ed Woodsum. Shortly thereafter Yale drove 43 yards in six plays for its third score.

But Harvard hadn't yielded yet. The Crimson pushed 50 yards to Yale's 10-yard line and then Clasby circled left end for the touchdown. Before Crimson fans could get excited, though, Molloy completed a deep pass to Frank Smith for 59 yards. Then he threw a 14-yard pass to Shears in the end zone. Bob Parsells kicked his third conversion and Yale led at the half, 27-7.

In the locker room underneath the stands, Charlie Yeager peeled off his clothes and looked for his uniform. Maybe the rout was on and he would be able to get into the game. He laced on his shoulder pads and slipped into the white football pants. He had no hip pads and there was no time to get his ankles taped. It was a struggle getting the blue Yale jersey over his shoulder pads, but he finally managed it. And as the team headed back to the field for the second half, Charlie Yeager put on his white helmet with the blue stripe and buckled the chin strap.

At the beginning of the third quarter, Molloy produced another Yale touchdown by connecting with Woodsum on a neatly executed 26-yard pass play. Now Olivar was looking up and down his bench. He wanted to give all of his boys a chance to play. He spotted Charlie, serious, intent on the game. "If we score again," Olivar called to him, "you go in for the extra point." Almost in disbelief, Yeager nodded.

Minutes later, Molloy threw another scoring

pass to Woodsum and right afterward team manager Charlie Yeager, number 99, was running out to line up against Harvard. When he reached the huddle, the players laughed. Molloy called the play, "We'll pass to Yeager from field-goal formation on the count of two."

Yeager crouched low at right end. As he moved forward, a big Harvard tackle charged right over him and knocked him to the ground. Charlie's hope for glory seemed about to disappear forever. Yale had faked the kick and now Molloy, seeing Yeager down, was running to his right. All of the other receivers were covered.

But Charlie wasn't through yet. He picked himself up and scooted for the end zone. Molloy spotted him and threw. Five yards into the end zone, Charlie turned and caught the ball against his stomach. It was Yale's 41st point of the game —and the first point that Charlie Yeager had ever scored.

In the radio booth above Harvard Stadium, the announcer was having trouble. There was no number 99 listed for Yale. He dispatched the Yale spotter, Stan Venoit, to the Yale bench. When Venoit arrived there, the players were mobbing Charlie and they lifted him quite easily to their shoulders. Venoit watched incredulously. "I wouldn't have believed it, Yeager," he screamed at Charlie, "unless I saw it right here."

After playing a memorable part in the 1952 Yale-Harvard
game, a beaming Charlie Yeager poses with a Yale teammate.

Venoit went back upstairs and soon the radio audience and the crowd received the announcement that the Yale manager, Charlie Yeager, had scored the extra point.

The final score was 41-14 and, though Molloy and Woodsum had been outstanding, the reporters crowded around Charlie Yeager, the diminutive Eli from Buffalo, New York.

"This was it. This was the greatest thrill in my life," he said.

With his one point, Charlie Yeager had fulfilled the dream of unsung college football managers everywhere.

9

The Longest Game

On December 23, 1962, as the crowd filled every available seat in Houston's Jeppessen Stadium and then overflowed into the aisles, several men were smiling with satisfaction. They were the same men who, three years earlier, had been ridiculed for organizing the American Football League. They had invested money in the belief that America could and would support two big pro football leagues. The National Football League still attracted the most attention, they admitted, but evidence of the success of their venture was right before their eyes—37,981 people had squeezed into the stands for the AFL championship game between the Dallas Texans and the Houston Oilers. And many millions were watching the game on television.

The young league obviously was on its way to success, and if one player could be considered particularly responsible, he was the Dallas Texan halfback—Abner Haynes.

From the beginning of the AFL's first season in 1960, Haynes had been the league's most prominent star. He had been an all-league halfback every year of its existence. In 1960 he had led the AFL in rushing and been picked as its Player of the Year. In 1961 he had scored a record five touchdowns in one game. In 1962 he had scored a record 19 touchdowns in one season. His popularity and importance were so overwhelming that after one game in Dallas the public-address announcer had said to the fans: "Please drive carefully on your way home. The life you save may be Abner Haynes'."

Haynes was especially important to the league because he had come to the AFL by choice, not in desperation. He had been drafted by the NFL, too. Therefore, no one could call Abner "an NFL reject," as some people called other AFL stars.

The December, 1962, game was Haynes' first championship game and he wanted it to be a showcase for his league. He and his coaches wanted the record crowd to see just how good the Dallas Texans really were. And he hoped to lead the team to victory with his swift and agile running and his acrobatic pass receiving.

Haynes weighed only 185 pounds and was just 5 feet 11 inches tall, but he was an incredibly skilled football player, and an electrifying one. When he played, he created excitement and attracted lavish praise. "But there's no sense in a runner getting big-headed," he had once said, "before he talks it over with his blockers."

Abner Haynes was a thoughtful, intelligent and courageous man. Following a spectacular schoolboy football career in Dallas, he had been offered several college scholarships. Instead he had chosen to enroll at his own expense at North Texas State, a college that had never before had a Negro athlete. He arrived at State, one of six Negro pioneers, and soon earned a football scholarship. He also earned All-America acclaim and, after his senior season in 1959, he made his decision in favor of the AFL and signed a pro contract with the Dallas Texans.

So, on December 23, 1962, Abner and the Texans were at the high point of their intertwined professional football careers—one victory away from a championship. The Texans stormed onto the field and proceeded to score a first-quarter field goal and two second-quarter touchdowns. At the half they led, 17-0.

Tommy Brooker had kicked the field goal and Haynes had scored the two touchdowns. He had scored the first on a 28-yard pass from quarterback Len Dawson, and the second on an intricate two-yard run.

In the second half, however, Houston scored 17 points and Dallas scored none. When time ran out, the score stood at a tie. Thus for the second time in pro football history, two tired and tense teams trudged to the sidelines to rest briefly before playing a sudden-death overtime. Everyone knew about the previous sudden-death game, in which Baltimore beat New York for the 1958 NFL championship. Everyone knew, too, that the rules for this one would be the same: the first team to score would win. A whole season would be settled on one play.

At the sidelines, Dallas coach Hank Stram talked with his offensive captain, Abner Haynes. They talked about the critical coin toss. The team that wins the toss has three choices: it can elect to receive, defend a specific goal or kick off. Many fans speculated on what the Texans would do if they won the toss. Would they choose to receive the kickoff? Or, since the wind was blowing in gusts of 14 miles an hour and more, would they choose to defend the goal that placed the wind at their backs? If they received the kickoff, they had a chance of scoring and winning the game before the Oilers even got their hands on the ball. On the other hand, after the Texans gained possession of the ball, the strong wind

Abner Haynes

would certainly carry the football a long way on
a field-goal attempt. And to win, a team needed
only a field goal. The wind also would help a
punt sail far, and a soaring punt would put the
opposing team deep in its own territory, nowhere near touchdown or field-goal range.

Stram told Abner that, if he won the toss, he
should choose the goal that would put the wind
at the Texans' back. Having the wind would be
more important than getting the football right

away. Of course, said Stram, if Houston won the toss and chose the wind advantage, Dallas would receive. Stram did not even consider the option to kick off. He wanted either the wind or the ball.

Abner ran onto the field, the referee flipped the coin and Abner called it correctly. It was his choice. "We'll kick to the clock," he said.

Unfortunately, Abner Haynes had blurted out his choice the wrong way. He had wanted to move his team toward the goal line in front of the clock. In that way, the wind would have been behind the players. But to make his plan work, he should have chosen to defend the goal at the opposite end of the field. Then the Oilers would obviously have elected to receive the ball, leaving the Texans to kick. But they would have been kicking in the direction Haynes actually intended.

By starting with the words, "We'll kick," Haynes had deprived his team of any choice of direction. All they had was the privilege of kicking. This, of course, left the Oilers with the obvious choice of defending the advantageous goal. Thus Haynes, by an unbelievable blunder, had left Dallas with no advantage at all. They wouldn't be receiving the football and they wouldn't have the wind behind them. If Houston could move the ball only a short way past midfield, then their expert kicker, George Blanda, could boom out a field goal.

The players on the field, the people in the stands, the people at television sets couldn't quite believe what Abner had done. A quick Houston field goal would make the fans forget the great record Abner had achieved over the years. Instead of talking about his touchdowns, his snaking runs, and his incredible pass receptions, people would remember only that his blunder had cost Dallas a championship.

Luckily, however, the Dallas defense held after the kickoff. In fact, the game stretched on, 17-17, through one 15-minute overtime period and into a second. With 2 minutes and 54 seconds gone in the second overtime, the Dallas kicker, Brooker, trotted onto the field to try a 25-yard field goal. As Brooker got ready to kick, he turned to fullback Curtis McClinton and smiled. "Don't worry, baby," Brooker said, confidently. "It's all over." Seconds later Brooker raced up to the football and kicked. The ball floated between the goal posts and over the crossbar—the Dallas Texans were champions.

From that moment the football game that might always have been remembered as "Haynes' Blunder," became known instead as "The Longest Game."

10

Sneaker Game

The 1934 Giant team had a number of great players. The quarterback was Ed Danowski, the skilled passer from Fordham University. Ken Strong, a fine kicker and runner, was the scoring leader. Mel Hein anchored the line at center. Ray Flaherty, the captain, caught the passes.

In 1933 the Giants had won their first division title, but had been defeated by the Bears in the play-off. Now, on December 9, 1934, the New York team was going to try again—against the Chicago Bears.

The morning of the fateful day, quarterback Danowski awoke early at his Riverhead, Long Island, home. The temperature was close to zero. The wind whistled through the streets and ice made walking and driving treacherous.

Jack Mara, president of the Giants, visited the Polo Grounds, where the game was to be played. After inspecting the field, he called Coach Steve Owen on the phone at his hotel in Manhattan.

"Steve," said Mara, "the field is frozen solid, just like a sheet of ice."

A few minutes later, at breakfast, Owen reported the sad news to Captain Ray Flaherty and tackle Bill Morgan.

"Why don't we wear sneakers?" asked Flaherty.

Flaherty had worn sneakers instead of football cleats in a college game in 1925. His team, gaining traction from the sneakers, had easily defeated their opponents.

"Great idea," said Owen. Then he frowned. "Where in the world do we get sneakers on Sunday?" he asked.

Owen, Flaherty and Morgan began calling sporting goods stores in Manhattan. None of them were open.

"It was a good idea," said Owen, gloomily, "but we won't be able to get them."

At the Polo Grounds the team was dressing. Owen walked out on the field, slipped on the ice and returned to the clubhouse in despair. The Giants would just have to play the Bears on slippery cleats.

Inside, trainers Gus Mauch and Charley Porter were taping ankles and talking to a little man named Abe Cohen. Abe made uniforms for Manhattan College and on Sundays hung around the Giants' dressing room. Because of his duties, he had a key to the Manhattan College supply room.

When Owen saw Abe, he had a sudden inspiration.

"Abe," said Owen, "could you get up to Manhattan College and get us some sneakers?"

Cohen was more than willing. He rushed out of the clubhouse, hailed a taxicab and raced uptown to Manhattan College.

In the stands 35,059 fans huddled under their blankets as the Giants, with their cleats, ran on the field.

"This is impossible," Danowski said to his teammates. "If I go back to pass I'll be down before I have a chance to lift my arm."

"Do the best you can," said Owen.

Strong kicked a field goal, giving the Giants a 3-0 lead. But the Bears, heavier and stronger, pushed the slipping New York team all over the field. Bronko Nagurski, the Bears' fullback, smashed over to score from the two-yard line. After Jack Manders converted, Chicago led, 7-3.

Then Manders kicked a field goal and the Bears led, 10-3, as the half ended. The Giants, frozen, slipping, and discouraged by battling the heavier Bears, trailed back to the clubhouse. Many of the players had broken cleats on their

Ken Strong converts for the Giants during the famous 1934 game with the Bears.

football shoes as a result of the hard, icy field.

While the Giant players were attempting to warm up, Abe Cohen pushed open the door. Dumping a box on the floor, he announced, "Nine pairs were all I could get."

Quickly the Giant players started to get into the sneakers.

Meanwhile the Bears' coach, George Halas, was grumbling about the delay. "What's holding them up?" he asked.

"They're changing into sneakers," somebody told Halas.

"Good," said Halas, "step on their toes."

The sneakers had little immediate effect. The Bears drove downfield again and Jack Manders kicked another field goal. Chicago now led, 13-3.

Suddenly, the sneakers started taking hold. Danowski faded to pass and his feet held firm. The pass was intercepted on the two, but the Giants' Ike Frankian grabbed the ball out of the defender's hands and jogged across the goal line in his sneakers. Strong converted, so that the Giants trailed by only three points.

The next series of plays clinched the game. Lou Little, the Columbia football coach and a friend of Owen's, had been watching from the press box. He had noticed that the Giants could beat the Bears on quicker moves. The sneakers gave them an edge.

"If you send Strong off-tackle he will be past the line before the Bears have a chance to grab him," Little said.

The ball went to Strong. He faked to his left, cut back sharply to his right and bounced off the referee. With his sneakers gripping the frozen ground, he outraced the Bears' secondary for a 42-yard touchdown. It put the Giants in the lead, 17-13.

"Right then," said Strong afterward, "we knew it was over. We could move and they couldn't."

Two minutes later Strong scored again on a reverse, a play nearly impossible on a frozen field. The sneakers made anything possible. Now the Giants led, 23-13, and the fans started pouring onto the field.

There were still five minutes left in the game when Danowski, running gingerly in his sneakers, cut inside the right end from the ten and scored again for the Giants. Bo Molenda converted and the Giants were the champions of the NFL. The final score was 30-13, with 27 points racked up in the final 15 minutes.

"They won it with the sneakers," said Bronko Nagurski, the saddened Bears' fullback. "They could cut back and we couldn't."

A little man with a mustache walked over to Ken Strong and stuck out his hand.

"Ken, I want to congratulate you," said Abe Cohen. "You played a wonderful game."

"Abe," said Strong, "you're the man who won this game. You deserve the write-ups."

Few people, alas, remember the name of Abe Cohen. But few football fans will ever forget the historic "Giants' sneaker game." It clinched an NFL championship for the Giants and, to Abe Cohen, the team's number one fan, that was more than enough.

11

Dream Team

Jerry Croyden picked up the phone in his office and dialed *The New York Times* in great excitement. As publicity man for Plainfield Teachers College, he was calling in the results of the school's latest victory. This time he reported that Plainfield had beaten Ingersoll, 13-0.

The rewrite man at the *Times* took the score and in the next day's paper the victory became a matter of record. This meant the third triumph for unbeaten Plainfield, whose previous victims had been Winona (27-0) and Randolph Tech (35-0).

During the 1941 season, Plainfield was on its way to a record that in some respects would be unequaled in the annals of college football.

Not only was Plainfield making the big city newspapers (the Philadelphia *Record*, among others), but its Chinese sophomore halfback, John Chung, was receiving special attention. After another Plainfield victory, Herbert Allan, sports writer for the New York *Post*, wrote in his "College Grapevine" column: "John Chung has accounted for 57 of the 98 points scored by his unbeaten and untied team in four starts. If the Jerseyans don't watch out, he may pop up in Chiang Kai-shek's offensive department one of these days."

Plainfield went on to add Scott and Chesterton to its list of conquests and with each victory Chung and his team gained in stature. The star halfback averaged, according to Croyden, 9.3 yards a carry. In one publicity release Croyden explained: "The prowess of Chung may be due to his habit of eating rice between the halves."

From all accounts, the future couldn't have been brighter for sophomore Chung and the Plainfield eleven. But suddenly things went wrong at Plainfield. On November 13, publicist Croyden sent out what proved to be his last press release: "Due to flunkings in the midterm examinations, Plainfield Teachers has been forced to call off its last two scheduled games with Appalachian Tech tomorrow and with Harmony Teachers on Thanksgiving Day. Among those thrown for a loss was John Chung, who has accounted for 69 of Plainfield's 117 points."

It was an abrupt finish for a team which might have even been invited to one of the smaller Bowl games on New Year's Day. But it was understandable in light of the surprising story which appeared in the November 17 issue of *Time* Magazine.

"For three weeks running," the account read, "the sports page of the New York *Times* has dutifully recorded the football victories of Plainfield (N.J.) Teachers College. The Philadelphia *Record* and other papers also took occasional notice of unbeaten Plainfield Teachers. The only error in all the reports . . . was that Plainfield and its opponents were nonexistent."

There was no Plainfield, no John Chung, no rice, no victories. Caswell Adams, a sports writer on the New York *Herald Tribune*, filled in the details of the great hoax. He discovered that the ghost team and its star halfback were dreamed up by a group of stockbrokers at Newburger, Loeb & Co., a Wall Street brokerage firm. The chief instigator of the hoax was Morris Newburger, an imaginative 35-year-old football fan.

Morris Newburger was Jerry Croyden. So were some of Morris' associates. On Saturday afternoons they would take turns calling the newspapers and manufacturing press releases about the marvelous feats of the team at Plainfield Teachers College.

For the stockbrokers this was certainly no money-making proposition. It was an investment in fun and fantasy. They wanted a winning football team and they got one.

They also received a tribute which Morris Newburger will always prize. It was a song written by *Herald-Tribune* reporter Cas Adams to the tune of Cornell's "High Above Cayuga's Waters":

> *Far above New Jersey's swamplands*
> *Plainfield Teachers' spires*
> *Mark a phantom, phony college*
> *That got on the wires.*
> *Perfect record made on paper*
> *Imaginary team!*
> *Hail to thee, our ghostly college,*
> *Product of a dream!*

12

Tuned In

As a football coach, Paul Brown was a genius. Everybody knew that, especially the men gathered around him at a preseason luncheon in 1957. They wondered what new tricks the master had up his sleeve this time. It seemed that every time the coach of the world-champion Cleveland Browns came up with a new play, or some fresh defensive wrinkle, other coaches would immediately adopt it for their own teams. Yet Brown always managed to stay one jump ahead of the others.

On this particular day he was holding a small object in his hand. When someone asked what it was, he explained that it was a receiving set.

"What's it for?" someone else asked.

"So I can talk to my quarterback during a game," said Brown.

As astonishing as the revelation seemed, it was nevertheless true. What Paul Brown unveiled that day was indeed a tiny radio receiving set that could fit snugly inside a football helmet. It was expressly made for the helmet of George Ratterman, a veteran quarterback who had taken over for the retired Otto Graham. The radio would enable Brown to stand on the sidelines with a microphone in his hands and tell his quarterback what plays to call in the huddle.

There was nothing new about Paul Brown's calling the plays; he had always called them in the past. But he had done it the hard way, by alternating his offensive guards on every play. He would send one in with the play on first down, then send in another guard with the next play, and so on. But now Brown could talk directly to his quarterback—if the radio worked.

As one of the luncheon guests said to Brown afterward, "Now you don't have to worry about your quarterback talking back to you. All he can do is listen."

Brown had worked out his plan very carefully. He had even obtained a citizens' band transmitter, which, in effect, gave him a small radio station on which he could broadcast plays to his quarterback.

The Cleveland Browns decided to test their new device in an exhibition game against the Detroit Lions in Akron, Ohio. And when the two teams took the field for the opening kickoff, the most worried man in the stadium was George Ratterman. The skies above him were darkening rapidly, and there was thunder and lightning. Ratterman, with his helmet wired for sound, was afraid he would be a walking lightning rod.

As soon as he began playing, however, he discovered that he had worse problems. The Lions had heard about Paul Brown's "radio station," and had decided they could kill the receiving set by kicking in Ratterman's helmet. Unfortunately Ratterman's head was inside the helmet, too. After absorbing a few hefty blows, the Browns' quarterback called time out and signaled to the Lion linemen.

"Look," he said, removing the helmet and dropping it on the ground heavily, "you can't destroy the radio this way. It takes a lot of punishment." And he slammed and bounced the helmet on the ground several times to make his point. But as soon as play started again, the Lions resumed their "headhunting."

Ratterman made another interesting discovery during the course of the game. He wasn't picking up Brown's signals clearly on every play. In order to get good reception, he had to step out-

Coach Paul Brown transmits instructions to his quarterback, George Ratterman.

side the huddle and rotate his body slowly, making a circle until he could read Brown loud and clear. "This is getting to be embarrassing," he said, as he stepped back into the huddle to announce the play Coach Brown had called from the sidelines.

The following week, the Browns played their final preseason exhibition game—against the Chicago Bears—in Chicago's Soldier Field. The game was a benefit for the Armed Forces, and a big halftime show had been scheduled. It required a great many last-minute preparations. During the game, the technicians who were in charge of setting up the various displays communicated with one another by walkie-talkie radio. Their signals clearly intruded on Brown's play calling. Each time Ratterman maneuvered his body to get a "fix" on Paul Brown's sideline instructions, he would pick up such comments as: "Charley, this is Bill. Move that float over more toward the 30-yard line. Yeah, that's right."

It was very disconcerting. After the game Ratterman said, "I couldn't hear a thing from the coach all day."

By the time the regular season began, Brown had decided not to employ his device against his opening-day opponent, the Chicago Cardinals. But the imitators were already at work. The Cardinals, for example, ran a wire antenna just under the turf of Comiskey Park and hooked it up to a transmitter. They equipped their quarterback and defensive captains with headsets inside their helmets. As a result, Coach Ray Richards was able to broadcast plays and instructions to his players throughout the game. The Cardinals beat the Browns, 9-7.

In the third week of the season, Cleveland had a home game scheduled with the Giants, who were coached by Jim Lee Howell. For this game Paul Brown decided to try his latest brainchild again. According to the Giants, however, the New York team came prepared with their own console receiver, which they set up next to the Giant bench.

By coincidence, the Giants had just picked up a player from the Browns—a halfback named Gene Filipski—who knew all the Browns' plays. As Paul Brown broadcast his plays to quarterback Ratterman, Filipski is supposed to have intercepted the transmission and decoded the play for Howell, who in turn gave instructions to his players on the field. Whether or not they actually had electronic aid that day, the Giants defeated the Browns, 21-9, giving Howell his very first victory over Cleveland.

In the Browns' dressing room after the game, an unhappy Paul Brown insisted that he had quit using the radio after the first few plays. Ratterman, he said, couldn't hear him above the roar of the more than 60,000 spectators. "There was just too much crowd noise," he explained.

In New York, however, the Giants' general manager, Ray Walsh, was saying, "We were able to get the Browns' signals better than they could. Finally, after three unsuccessful series of plays, they gave it up.

It didn't really matter very much whose story was more accurate because, shortly afterward, National Football League Commissioner Bert Bell banned the use of all radio devices in football helmets. Everyone in football seemed to agree that the ruling was for the good of the sport.

But it is interesting to speculate on just how far the electronic gadgetry and intrigue might have gone without the commissioner's ruling. The fans would probably have enjoyed the spectacle of Martian-like players with antennae sprouting from their helmets.

13

Wrong-Way Runners

A person without much knowledge of football history would have little reason to connect Roy Riegals with Jim Marshall, other than the fact that they both played football. First of all, they were born 30 years apart. Riegels grew up on the West Coast, Marshall in the Midwest. Riegels was white, Marshall a Negro. Riegels went to the University of California, Marshall to Ohio State. Riegels' football career ended in college, while Marshall became a standout in the pros. And even their personalities were direct opposites. There was nothing unusual about the quiet Riegels, but the flamboyant Marshall loved to laugh and longed for adventure.

Yet, despite their many differences, Riegels

and Marshall will be forever linked in football history. They share an identical moment of agony, when each wished he could have been swallowed up by the earth of the playing field. And they also share the rare knowledge that no matter how colossal the mistake a person makes, it will affect him only as much as he permits it to.

The story of the common bond between Riegels and Marshall began on New Year's Day, 1929. Georgia Tech was playing California in the Rose Bowl, and the game appeared to be a big mismatch. California had finished second in the Pacific Coast Conference and had been chosen for the Rose Bowl only because champion Southern Cal was at odds with the Rose Bowl committee. Georgia Tech, on the other hand, had given up just 40 points all season and took a 9-0 record into the game.

The game turned out to be a good deal closer than most people had predicted. And by the time it ended, 66,404 spectators had witnessed one of the most bizarre contests ever played. At one point the football collapsed after a punt. On another play California's Benny Lom grabbed a fumble in mid-air and dashed 68 yards for the touchdown, only to have the referee rule that the play was dead because the forward progress of the ball had been stopped. There was even a kickoff from the wrong yard line. And, finally,

California's Lee Rice, who was wearing a new pair of shoes with a cleat near the toe, stumbled on a clod of earth just as he was in the clear and about to catch a pass.

As wild as all these things were, they have been obscured over the years by what took place early in the second quarter. The game was still scoreless and Georgia Tech had the ball, first down and ten yards to go, on their own 25-yard line. Tailback Stumpy Thomason took the snapback and headed for an opening between left end and left tackle. Thomason had gone about five yards when a tackler hit him around the ankles. He went down and the ball squirted from his arms.

Riegels, playing a roving center for California, had drifted with the play parallel to the line of scrimmage. The ball landed in front of him and he scooped it up. He began running toward the Georgia Tech goal line, but spotted two Tech players coming at him from the right. To avoid them he made a horseshoe turn, and completely lost his bearings. Instead of turning back toward the Tech goal line, he began running for his own end zone.

Benny Lom was the first California player to realize what Riegels was doing. He began chasing his teammate down the left sideline. Normally he would have caught him after 30 or 40

Roy Riegels races 70 yards to his own goal during the 1929 Rose Bowl game between the University of California and Georgia Tech.

yards, but Riegels had a huge head start and was probably running faster than ever before. He was intent on scoring a touchdown—a big event in any lineman's life.

Afraid that he would reach Riegels too late, Lom began yelling, "Stop, stop! You're going the wrong way. Throw me the ball."

At first Riegels couldn't hear Lom because of the roar of the crowd. When he finally did hear him, Riegels caught only the part about throwing the ball. "After running all this way," Riegels thought to himself, "I'll be darned if I'm going to let him score the touchdown."

Riegels had crossed the ten-yard line before Lom was finally able to grab his right arm, trying desperately to stop him from crossing the goal. Like a cowboy bulldogging a steer, Lom held on to Riegels, finally stopping him and swinging him around at the one-yard line. Both men stood still for a moment and Riegels at last realized his error. But before he could begin the long trek upfield, a wave of Tech players swarmed on top of him, driving him into the end zone. The referee, however, signaled that the play had ended on the one-yard line.

California went into a huddle; and no one said a word except for giving Lom the order to punt the ball. Lom stood as far back in the end zone as possible, but it was not far enough. Two Tech

After realizing his error, Riegels (hand on head) sits dejectedly among his teammates.

defenders broke through to partially block the kick. The ball went straight up in the air and was caught by California's Stan Barr for a safety.

Georgia Tech's unexpected two points went on to provide Tech's margin of victory. The final score was Georgia Tech 8, California 7. But the real story of the game was neither Tech's victory nor Riegels' horrible mistake. It was the way

Riegels shook off his misery to play a second half that may have been the finest 30 minutes of football in his life. "Some would have folded after what he did," said Georgia Tech All-America center Peter Pund. "Roy was a battler who never quit."

Riegels had another year of eligibility and was elected captain of the 1929 California team —not out of sympathy, but in tribute to his leadership abilities and his courage. He even gained All-America mention that year.

In the years that followed, Riegels was first a successful high-school coach and then a successful businessman. His name also became synonymous with an error in direction. If an athlete went the wrong way on the playing field, he was said to be "doing a Riegels."

Naturally there were instances of players running the wrong way in high-school and small-college games through the years. But not until October 25, 1964, did anyone have to suffer the same glare of nationwide publicity as Roy Riegels.

The Minnesota Vikings of the National Football League were playing the San Francisco 49ers in San Francisco. Carl Eller of the Vikings had just scooped up a 49er fumble and turned it into a touchdown. Working hard to get back the touchdown, 49er quarterback George Mira threw a short pass into the secondary to halfback Bill Kilmer. Jim Marshall of the Vikings quickly diagnosed the play and headed for Kilmer. Marshall got there quickly, demonstrating the speed that had prompted his coach, Norm Van Brocklin, to call him "the fastest animal I have ever seen on a pro football line."

Someone hit Kilmer and the 49er halfback fumbled. Reacting instinctively, Marshall hurdled a player in front of him and, on the run, picked up the loose ball. Without hesitation he began sprinting for the goal line—the Minnesota goal line—66 yards away.

Like Riegels, Marshall had simply gotten mixed up. And the roar of the crowd drowned out his teammates' shouts. Marshall ran into the end zone without opposition. He began to realize that something was wrong when San Francisco's Bruce Bosely threw his arms around him, thanking him for the safety. Then Viking quarterback Fran Tarkenton ran up and said, "Jim, you went the wrong way, the wrong way."

Marshall buried his head in his hands for a few anguished moments and then jogged back to the bench. Coach Van Brocklin, a man with a notoriously short temper, realized that the situation was not one that called for angry words. He smacked Marshall on the backside and said, "For-

Left: After scooping up a San Francisco fumble, Minnesota's Jim Marshall gets confused and begins a 66-yard run into his own end zone. Right: Finally realizing the result of his run, Marshall tries to hide his head in shame.

get about it, Jim. Go back in there and make the fans forget."

For the rest of the game Marshall played excellent football. And the fact that Minnesota won, 27-22, helped minimize the damage Marshall's two-point safety had caused.

After the game, Marshall was naturally concerned about the possible effects the incident would have on his reputation. But he needn't have worried. He received thousands of sympathetic letters and cards, advising him not to let the mistake depress him. Most cherished of all was a letter from Roy Riegels, telling him to treat the incident with humor.

For Marshall, a quick-witted fellow with an appreciation for the unusual, Riegels' advice wasn't at all difficult to follow. Jim worked up a funny little talk about his experience and found himself in great demand at banquets all around the country.

It takes an exceptional person to shrug off a huge mistake and turn it into an advantage. Both Riegels and Marshall carried it off with great dignity, proving their worth off the field as well as on it.

14

Lonely End

As Army went into the last game of the 1957 season, the Cadets appeared to be headed toward an extremely successful year. They had lost their third game of the season, a tough 23-21 defeat at the hands of a strong Notre Dame team, but five victories had followed. Then on that last Saturday, in Philadelphia's Municipal Stadium, more than 100,000 fans watched Navy beat Army, 14-0. The fact that Navy was Army's bitter rival made the defeat even more painful.

"That's the game you think about all winter," said Earl "Red" Blaik, the Army coach.

As a result of the defeat, Colonel Blaik set about devising a new offensive strategy. In 1958 Army would be strong again, but so would

Navy. Blaik wanted to have a good season, of course. But even more important, he wanted Army to avenge its loss.

In Colonel Blaik's strategy one man played a crucial role. He was a previously undistinguished end named William Stanley Carpenter. As a sophomore in 1957, Carpenter had been injured and had seen action in just four games. Bob Anderson, an All-America halfback, and Pete Dawkins were the leaders of the team. In fact, not too many people outside of Carpenter's close friends knew that Bill was even on the team.

"He was a good cadet who liked the spit and polish of West Point life," Anderson said.

Besides being a diligent cadet, the 6-foot 2-inch, 205-pound Carpenter was a fine lacrosse player.

"I needed a player who was strong, smart and agile. Most of all he had to be able to handle the possible pressures," Colonel Blaik said.

On September 27, 1958, Blaik's new tactics were revealed for the first time. Army was playing South Carolina, a weak team, so the Cadets had a chance to experiment before the later, more important games.

Joe Caldwell, the Cadet quarterback, came on the field for the first play, and the offense lined up in front of him for the play call and the signal

number. They bent down and listened to his call.
But the spectators noticed something odd—one
player wasn't in the huddle. He was 15 yards
away from the huddle, his hands on his hips, his
eyes glued to the movement of the Army quarterback.

The reporters in the press box at Army's
Michie Stadium scanned their program. The detached player was number 87, end Bill Carpenter.

Throughout the game, by some mysterious
method, Carpenter was able to follow the play,
decide if it was a pass or run, and carry out his
assignment without going near the huddle. His
uncanny ability upset the South Carolina defense, and served as a psychological weapon.

"ARMY USES LONELY END" headlined the newspaper the day after the Cadets overwhelmed
South Carolina, 45-8. Under Blaik's leadership,
Army went on to beat Penn State, Notre Dame
and Virginia. Then Army was tied by Pittsburgh, 14-14. After that, in quick succession,
Colgate, Rice and Villanova went down to defeat. And finally the Cadets gained their revenge
on Navy for the 1957 loss.

Carpenter was the big story of the year. How
did he get his signals? Who told him where to
run on plays? What could the defense do to
stop him?

His classmates at West Point kidded him about

"Lonely End," Bill Carpenter (87), remains 15 yards away as Army teammates go into their huddle.

staying away from the huddle, suggesting that the real cause might be bad breath.

The "Lonely End," who wasn't really lonely at all with that amount of attention, was collecting fan mail by the sackful.

"Most of it," he said, "came from girls. They all volunteered to be my friend. I even got some letters from Lonely Hearts clubs."

In January of 1959, Colonel Blaik, who was retiring from West Point, revealed the details of his Lonely End strategy at a dinner of the Touchdown Club of New York. He began by explaining the complicated signal system.

"Caldwell [the quarterback] signals Carpenter with his feet. Two feet together means a run; left out front, also a run; right foot out front, a pass. Carpenter then signals Caldwell by rubbing his nose or tugging on his helmet. That revealed where he should run."

The audience was shocked at the explanation.

"Simple, wasn't it?" said Blaik.

"It was so simple I should have thought of it," said Eddie Erdelatz, the Navy coach.

The secret of the Lonely End was out. All the opposing coaches knew what to watch for, and everyone imagined that Carpenter would have to come back into the huddle.

In 1959, Dale Hall, a former Army quarterback, took over as head coach. The football coaches of other schools could scarcely wait for Army's first game, against Boston College.

With the first offensive play, Carpenter, now a senior and the team captain, moved out 15 yards. Surprisingly, he would play his solitary role again. But it was thought that since opposing teams knew how he got his signals, he would be easily stopped. Boston College failed to do so, however. In that game Carpenter caught nine passes for 140 yards and two touchdowns.

For the next six games, Carpenter caught passes, blocked, and led the team in yards gained. Then in the Villanova game, he suffered a dislocated shoulder. This meant he would probably be sitting on the bench for the game against Oklahoma. Instead, his shoulder was strapped to his body and he caught six passes for 67 yards as Army was defeated by a close 28-20. Carpenter ended his football career in the game against Navy. Although the Middies won, 43-12, they couldn't stop the Lonely End. He caught four passes for 93 yards and a touchdown.

In June of 1960, Carpenter graduated from West Point and the Lonely End era was over. He had been picked for every major All-America team and had established five pass-catching records. He had also been appointed a cadet battalion commander and had won a special award for "Inspirational Personal Courage" in athletics. His old coach, Colonel Blaik, said, "Bill Carpenter has the mentality for doing the unusual. He will make a fine officer."

"Someday," predicted his teammate Bob Anderson, "Bill Carpenter will be Army Chief of Staff."

Six years later, in Vietnam, for the heroic rescue of the men under his command, Captain William Carpenter was awarded the Silver Star and recommended for the Congressional Medal of Honor.

15

The Praying Colonels

Centre College is a small Presbyterian school located in Danville, Kentucky. It was founded in the early 1800s. Most people have never heard of it, and that's not surprising. Throughout its history Centre has never had more than 700 students. Yet there was a time when Centre's football team was the equal of any in the country. And by winning one game in particular—a victory that has been called "the biggest upset of the half-century"—tiny Centre helped to change the course of college football in the United States.

In 1916 a number of Centre alumni decided that their old school should be as distinguished in football as it was in other fields. The school had produced two Vice-Presidents of the United

States, a Supreme Court justice, eight United States senators, 10 governors and 20 college presidents. But never, sad to say, had there been an All-America football player. So Robert "Chief" Myers, a Centre alumnus himself, was hired as coach and ordered to turn Centre's dreams of football glory into reality.

Myers began the seemingly impossible task by bringing with him five players he had coached to an undefeated season at a Fort Worth, Texas, high school. These players amounted to almost half a team, for in those days it was not uncommon to see 11 men play an entire game. Then Myers started searching throughout Kentucky for other players. In a letter he described the kind of athlete he was seeking:

"We want nice boys who are willing to take an anvil in each hand and fight a shark at the bottom of the ocean or ride a porcupine without a saddle. If you find a likely prospect, put a rope around his neck and lead him in."

Recruiting, along with his other tasks, kept Myers so busy that in the fall of 1917 he turned over the coaching job to "Uncle Charlie" Moran. Until then, Uncle Charlie had been a National League baseball umpire. But he was the ideal man for the Centre job. He knew football and, just as important, he was aware of the value of publicity. Both he and Myers realized that no matter how well Centre played, the team would somehow have to capture the public's attention in order to get invitations to play big-time schools.

It was not long before Moran's hopes were realized and Centre suddenly became an object of nationwide interest. During the halftime of Centre's 1917 game against Kentucky, Moran was giving the team a stirring pep talk. Suddenly he stopped in the middle of his talk. "Boys," he said, "I suppose I've been what some folks would call a rough cuss, but I've played the game of life straight. . . . I believe in God, and I'm sure He looks after folks who are doing their best." He paused, and then, looking at the floor, said, "Boys, won't one of you say a word of prayer?"

There were several seconds of silence. Then a big lineman named Bob Mathias jumped up and began to pray. When Mathias had finished, nearly every man on the team was praying.

Centre won the game, 3-0. Newspapers reported the incident widely, labeling the Centre team "The Praying Colonels." Soon the team achieved a colorful reputation that was circulated all around the country.

Centre was unbeaten in 1917. The following year there was no football because of World War I. But in 1919 The Praying Colonels were undefeated again, with a 14-6 victory over West Vir-

Captain Bo McMillin and Coach "Uncle Charlie" Moran of Centre College.

ginia which thrust them squarely into the foot-ball spotlight.

That triumph brought them an invitation to play the great Harvard team in 1920. And it also brought Centre three All-America mentions from famed selector Walter Camp. Center Red Weaver and quarterback Bo McMillin both made the first team and Jim "Red" Roberts, an end, was named to the third team.

The Praying Colonels warmed up for their big

game with Harvard by routing Morris Harvey College (66-0), Howard University (120-0), and Transylvania College (55-0). But the game with Harvard was not nearly as easy. Centre managed to hold the Crimson to a 14-14 tie at halftime, but in the next half two of Centre's passes were intercepted and turned into Harvard touchdowns. Final score: Harvard 31, Centre 14.

Still, The Praying Colonels had nothing to be ashamed of. They had displayed a quick and courageous brand of football. At game's end, a Harvard player picked up the ball and handed it to quarterback McMillin. "Here," he said, "you deserve it." "Thank you," said McMillin, returning the ball, "but next year we'll be back, and we'll win it on our own."

For a year the Centre team lived only for the Harvard rematch. And, according to plan, they were back at Harvard on October 29, 1921. But they appeared to have no more chance of winning than they had had the previous year. Harvard, the citadel of college football, was fresh from a 28-game winning streak. And it hadn't lost an intersectional contest in 44 years.

During the first half the bigger Harvard team predictably dominated the play; yet neither team had scored by intermission. Then, early in the third quarter, entirely without warning, there occurred one of the most dramatic plays in foot-

Bo McMillin completes a pass during Centre's historic 1920 game with Harvard.

ball history. Centre lined up at the Harvard 32 in an unbalanced line to the right. Tailback Mc-Millin took the snapback. He followed his interference until he was almost out of bounds on the right sideline. As all the Harvard defenders headed his way, Bo suddenly switched directions. Only two Harvard backs could reverse themselves in time to have any chance to cut off the swift tailback. They ran toward him at an angle, trying to cut him off as he headed for the other corner of the field and the goal line.

Bo made it past the 15-yard line, then the 10, and once again he was nearly out of bounds. This time, instead of changing directions, he simply stopped. One defender overshot him. The second Harvard player grabbed at Bo's elbow, but couldn't hang on. Bo dashed into the end zone. Centre missed the extra point, but led, 6-0.

After that, Centre threatened twice more to score—but without success. As the late-October shadows fell over the stadium, the rugged play began to tell on the lighter Centre team. But the clock was on their side. Harvard's last chance to avoid defeat was crushed when Centre's 158-pound fullback, Long Tom Bartlett, intercepted a pass with less than a minute left. The Praying Colonels ran out the clock and after the gun had sounded they stood on the field in stunned silence for a few moments. Then, as they realized what they had done, they began dancing in little circles, shouting, "We've won, we've beaten them."

The nation quickly learned the story of how this little school, whose total number of students was considerably less than the number of professors at Harvard, had emerged triumphant. It was a victory for the little guy everywhere, and it marked the beginning of a distinct change in the nature of college football. The colorful Praying Colonels attracted a new breed of fan to the game. These new fans poured into stadiums all over the country in record numbers. No longer was Eastern football the "only" football.

Ironically, though, little Centre could not keep up with the expenses as the game began to grow. Soon the team fell back into the same class of football that was played by Morris Harvey and Transylvania. But the one thing that Centre College can never lose is its very special place in the classic "David and Goliath" football legend.

16

Return of Bronko

In 1937 Bronko Nagurski turned in his Chicago Bear uniform and formally retired from professional football. At that time he told George Halas, the owner and coach of the Bears, to call on him if the team ever needed help. Six years later Nagurski regretted having uttered those words.

In 1943 the Second World War was ravaging Europe and the Pacific and the Bears were being whittled down by the call-up of their able-bodied men. They were gradually becoming a team of old-timers, veterans in their late thirties, and young rookies, just out of college, who hadn't received their draft notices yet. In addition, Coach Halas was serving in the U. S. Navy, so the Bears were deprived of his brilliant coaching.

As a result, the Chicago team indeed needed help, and Halas did not hesitate to put pressure on Nagurski to keep his promise. Finally, after much persuasion, Bronko agreed to come out of retirement.

Most football people felt that, if anyone could step back into the grueling role of a pro-football player after an absence of six years, the fabled Nagurski could do it. Nagurski had played for the University of Minnesota from 1927 to 1929 and was considered the greatest fullback ever to come out of college. In his senior year he received more votes as an All-America at tackle than he did at fullback. In 1930 he joined the Bears, and for the next eight years was the most destructive ball carrier in the National Football League.

Nagurski had become a legend, and after six years of retirement the legend would be trying to make a comeback.

Nagurski reported to the Bears' camp only a couple of days before their 1943 season opener with Green Bay. The Bears' co-coaches, Hunk Anderson and Luke Johnsos, had decided that Nagurski would fit in best at tackle, but he didn't know any of the signals. He had to take a cram course to learn them before game time. Luckily, he had kept himself in good shape, so he didn't take long in getting back into condition. His most immediate need was to build up his wind and endurance.

His old roommate, guard George Musso, was still with the Bears, and each day after practice he would talk Bronko into taking an extra lap or two around the field. Aside from Musso, however, there weren't many of the old crowd left. Danny Fortmann, the other guard, was there, and so was right halfback Ray Nolting, but most of the other players were new faces. The club was quarterbacked by a youngster from Columbia named Sid Luckman.

Although the Bears were worn thin by the wartime draft, they still had a good chance to win the Western Division crown. Their toughest opposition would probably come from the Packers, so the opening game would be a good test for the Bears. It would also serve as a trial for Nagurski's comeback.

He started the game at tackle, playing both offense and defense. The game was only a few minutes old when Nagurski, down in his stance, heard an opposing lineman remark, "Hey Nagurski, I thought they put you out to pasture with the rest of the old war horses."

"Save your wind, kid," Nagurski growled back. "You may need it later."

Bronko played like anything but an old retread. Luckman showed he had faith in him by

The Chicago Bears' backfield pose before the 1943 championship game with the Washington Redskins: (left to right) Dante Magnani, Harry Clark, Bronko Nagurski and Sid Luckman. Behind them, a canvas tarpaulin protects the field from snow.

running plays over his tackle position. Nagurski opened the holes for Bill Osmanski, Harry Clark, Gary Famiglietti, Dante Magnani and any of the other Bear ball carriers Luckman called on. It was ironic that Nagurski, once the mightiest ball carrier of all, was now relegated to the role of blocker, but Bronko took to his new duties with a fury.

He was more effective on offense than on defense. It was easy for him to remove an enemy defender with a hefty cross block, but he had difficulty understanding the new defensive tactics that had been added to the game during his six-year absence. In a game against the Giants, he played especially badly on defense and took himself out of the game. "They're running right over me," he told Anderson as he came to the sidelines. "Better send somebody else in."

Somehow, the Bears put a winning season together and Nagurski managed to drag his tired, 35-year-old body onto the football field for nine consecutive Sundays. As the season went into its final week, the Bears were in first place with a record of seven wins, one loss and one tie. The Packers were only one game behind them in the standings. The Bears needed to win their final game, against their crosstown rivals, the Chicago Cardinals, to clinch the Western Division title.

On the train taking them back from Washington, where they had just been beaten by the Redskins, 21-7, the Bears counted their injured players. "There's not a healthy fullback in the house," remarked Assistant Coach Phil Handler. Then somebody suggested that they use Nagurski at fullback for the last game.

Bronk was sitting alone and staring out the window at the bleakness of the passing landscape. "How would you like to play a little fullback next Sunday?" Hunk Anderson asked him. Nagurski looked up as though someone had just exploded a firecracker beside him. Then he sank deeper into his seat and resigned himself to the inevitable. "All right," he said, "time is running short, but anything for the club."

"Old number three is being rolled back on the track," a newspaper reported after the Bears announced Sunday's lineup. Indeed, Nagurski seemed to creak like a rusty train as he spent the week trying to polish up the line-crashing style he had taken years to perfect. It wasn't easy handling the tricky hand-offs from the quarterback and then storming the line—not after six years of retirement. But he worked hard at his offensive tactics, and by Sunday he said that he was as ready as he would ever be.

Nagurski was on the bench when the game started. The Bears planned to get along without him for as long as they could. The score seesawed back and forth in the first half. Then the Cardinals scored two touchdowns in the second period to take a 24-14 halftime lead.

There was no scoring in the third period, and as the fourth quarter began, the Bears' chances appeared to be fading rapidly. The period was scarcely two minutes old when the Bears were stalled on what had looked like a promising drive. They had a fourth down and four yards to go on the Cardinal 33. At that point, Nagurski came off the bench and went into the game at fullback.

Fourth-down plays were invented for men like Nagurski, and these were the situations Nagurski understood best. Clearly his time had come. He took the hand-off from Luckman and his 228-pound frame exploded into the line. The Cardinal line gave six yards, and the Bears had their precious first down. A moment later Luckman passed to Clark for a touchdown, and the Bears were back in the game.

Nagurski stayed in the game on offense. Every time Luckman needed a first down, he handed the ball to his fullback, and Bronko got the necessary yardage. With Nagurski bucking and Luckman passing, the Bears came from behind to win, 35-24.

In the title game against the Washington Redskins, Nagurski was asked to play his crucial role one last time. The Bears needed his pulverizing running to grind out the first downs. And again, Nagurski came through. When Chicago needed two yards, Bronko produced them, sometimes with yards to spare. At least five times during the game, the Bears were faced with crucial fourth-down plays, and each time Bronko delivered the necessary yardage. The Bears rolled up a 41-21 victory to win the championship.

For Nagurski it had been a laborious year, if not a brilliant one. He had done his job well, a spectacular achievement for a player after a six-year layoff. The record book credits him with 85 yards on 16 carries during the last two games of the season, and they were probably the hardest yards he ever earned.

They were the last, too. After the game, he retired again. "It's not a game for 35-year-old men," he said. "I can't listen to George Halas' songs all my life."

17

Who Needs to Practice?

The American Football League's New York Jets would like to forget that there once was a team called the New York Titans, a remarkable outfit that dissolved into bankruptcy after the 1962 season. This was the team that reappeared in 1963 as the Jets.

The owner of the Titans was Harry Wismer, a former radio broadcaster, who was known for his changing moods. Once, when a future opponent asked for pictures of the Titans to help publicize an upcoming game, Mr. Wismer sent 100 portraits of himself.

The Titans operated on an unusual schedule. AFL rules specify that a team must arrive for a road game at least 24 hours before the kickoff.

But the Titans often left home for the next day's game late at night so the club wouldn't have to buy dinner for the players.

Another league rule specifies that players must be paid within 24 hours after a game. Most teams pay their men in the clubhouse minutes after the final whistle. The Titans, however, often had to wait and wait. During the 1962 season this particular problem led to a great deal of trouble.

For two years the club had been coached by Sammy Baugh, the tall, lean former passing star. Baugh acted as a firm-willed buffer between the front office and the long-suffering players. But by the start of the 1962 season, Baugh had been fired. He was replaced by Bulldog Turner, a big former all-pro center.

Trouble began in San Diego when the Titans lost their fourth straight pre-season exhibition game, 14-9. AFL players are supposed to get $50 for each exhibition game they play, but because Wismer was angry no checks were forthcoming. The players, who were staying out on the West Coast to open the season against the Oakland Raiders the following week, were angry, too.

Lee Riley and Bob Mischak, the player representatives, went to George Sauer, who doubled as backfield coach and general manager. Sauer suggested that the players get in touch with AFL Commissioner Joe Foss if they did not receive their money. But he also recommended that they be patient with the club for a while. "You'll get paid," he promised.

Stranded more than 2,000 miles from home, the players had to follow his advice. Two or three days later the situation brightened again when a strong-armed quarterback named Lee Grosscup joined the squad. In the game against Oakland, Grosscup threw two long touchdown passes and the Titans scored a 28-17 upset. Wismer was pleased with the Titans' performance and, since he had received his guarantee check from the Raiders, everybody was paid.

The celebration didn't last very long, however. On Tuesday the Titans moved down to San Diego. It was a bad week. The bus company that transported the players to and from their practices hadn't been paid for the previous year, so the drivers left the players stranded at their distant practice field. Then on Sunday the Titans were murdered by the Chargers, 40-14. Wismer was red-faced with anger. He severely criticized the players, accusing them of not trying.

Later, a completely beaten group of players was herded onto a midnight flight to New York. They arrived about seven o'clock Monday morning and were informed that there was to be no practice that day. But a little later, when some of the players wandered down to the Titan office to pick up their checks, they were told the checks weren't quite ready.

The next morning, Tuesday, the Titans gathered at the campus of New York University, where they would practice for a week until the baseball Mets vacated the Polo Grounds. The Titans' next game was to be played on Saturday night in Buffalo. There was some buzzing about the late checks and still more complaining when Turner, under Wismer's orders, scheduled a heavy contact drill in full equipment. Wismer watched the practice, then left the field without saying anything. The players called a meeting as soon as the workout ended.

The locker rooms at NYU were on the third floor of the gym. Some players sat on the few stools, others sprawled on the floor and more perched on rolled-up wrestling mats. Mischak, an impressive-looking West Point graduate and all-league guard, called the meeting to order. Several players suggested going along with the club, knowing that the checks would eventually be forthcoming. But the veterans had been through this once too often. The season was opening, and they needed money to bring their families to New York and set up housekeeping. They voted to give the club a deadline of noon on Wednesday.

"No checks, no practice," Larry Grantham,

an all-star linebacker and team leader, told Sauer.

But the checks are coming," Sauer pleaded.

"Yeah, so's Christmas," Grantham replied.

"Regardless of whether we win or lose, we're still supposed to get paid," Mischak told Coach Turner. Later, one of the players called the league office in Dallas to report the situation.

The Titans had scheduled a press day on Wednesday for players to pose for pictures and be available for interviews. Turner pleaded with them to make an appearance while the writers were around. "The money will be here at noon," he promised. But noon came and the checks hadn't arrived. The players left the field even though Bulldog begged them to stay.

By one o'clock the checks finally arrived at NYU, but by this time the players were dressed and it was too late for the day's workout. Unfortunately, the week was a "short" one, too, because the Titans were playing Saturday night instead of Sunday.

But now, hard on the heels of the unprecedented one-day strike, came the most unbelievable stroke of all. Wismer decided that if the players wouldn't practice, then he would make sure that his coaches didn't coach! Late Wednesday night, Sauer received a telegram from Wismer, stating that the coaches were not to participate in practice or they would violate their contracts.

When the Titans gathered at NYU the next morning, Turner read them a similar telegram and then retreated to his office. Sauer called the squad together. The players trusted him and he felt obligated to try to save everyone from grief. "You see what a lousy situation this is getting to be," he told them. "Well, I just think you have too much pride in your abilities as football players to continue like this. Go out on the field and have the best practice you ever had."

The players reacted to Sauer's pep talk. Mischak called the offensive players aside while Grantham and Riley, a safetyman, took charge of the defense. The little groups discussed the upcoming game and talked over the Buffalo Bills' strengths and weaknesses they recalled from previous games. The players worked up a tentative game plan, then charged out on the field to practice for 90 minutes. They later agreed that it was the best practice they had had all year.

Sauer, in street clothes, watched discreetly from a distance. Wismer, of course, showed up to see if the coaches had followed his orders.

Because Saturday's game was so close, the players' game plan had to be used against Buffalo. On Friday the team arrived in Buffalo. And on Saturday night they trotted onto the worn turf of Buffalo's War Memorial Stadium as two-touchdown underdogs. The 24,000 Buffalo fans in the stadium had been reading of strange events in New York City and they expected an easy victory.

Buffalo took the opening kickoff and drove downfield, but Riley, who was to tie the league's interception record that season, intercepted a pass in the end zone to kill the threat. Shortly afterward, Buffalo quarterback Al Dorow was injured.

At this point the Titan offense began to move. The players' game plan had called for Grosscup to throw short passes and he did so with deadly effect. With the ball on the Bills' four-yard line, Dick Christy slipped off tackle for a touchdown.

Before the half, Grosscup completed a short pass to right end Thurlow Cooper for another score and the Titans left the field with a 14-6 advantage. They couldn't help looking up at the owner's box with wry smiles on their faces.

The second half was completely dominated by the Titan defense. Buffalo never really threatened to score, and Bill Shockley kicked a 35-yard field goal to complete the 17-6 upset.

Buffalo fans were enraged. They showered empty beverage cans on their beaten Bills as the players left the field. Some of the missiles also

After making a large gain, the Titans' Dick Christy is brought down by Buffalo defensemen.

bounced off the Titans' helmets, but they didn't care. They had showed up Wismer and, more important, they had vindicated their pride in themselves. Mischak spoke for the team: "Remember, we'd had two 7-7 seasons under Baugh and we considered ourselves pretty good football players. By winning as we did, we showed what we could accomplish with just a little organization. It was a delightful conclusion."

For a week, at least, the complicated game of professional football had been returned to the players. The following week the coaches took over again, and New York lost to a pitiful Denver team, 32-10.

18

A Kind of Justice

Neither Notre Dame nor Syracuse had a chance to win the national championship, but that fact made their meeting at South Bend, Indiana, on November 18, 1961, no less important. For Syracuse, which had won six and lost two, there was the hope of an invitation to a big New Year's Day bowl game. And for Notre Dame there was simply its football pride—a victory would be a big enough prize for the Fighting Irish and their fans. Notre Dame had suffered through two straight losing seasons and now, going into the Syracuse game, its record was 4-3. A victory over Syracuse, with two more games left to play, would assure at least a .500 season, if not better.

It would be difficult to say which team was the favorite. Syracuse had the better record and it also had halfback Ernie Davis. Davis was already considered a cinch to win the 1961 Heisman Trophy as America's best college football player. But Syracuse's schedule couldn't compare to Notre Dame's. In their first three games the Fighting Irish had beaten Oklahoma, Purdue and Southern Cal—three teams that are consistently tough opponents. And two of Notre Dame's three defeats could just as easily have gone the other way. Notre Dame had lost an extremely close game to Northwestern, 12-10. They followed that with an equally agonizing 13-10 loss to Navy.

Comparison scores didn't offer much of a clue to the game's probable outcome. The two teams had had just one opponent in common—the University of Pittsburgh. Syracuse had won, 28-9, and Notre Dame had won, 26-20. After every possible bit of pregame information had been sifted and analyzed, only one conclusion was possible: The game was going to be close.

A crowd of 49,246 were on hand at Notre Dame Stadium. After sitting through a scoreless first quarter, they roared with delight when Notre Dame finally scored. With the ball on the Syracuse 41-yard line, sophomore quarterback Frank Budka went back to pass. He found Angelo Dabiero open, and Dabiero went all the way for the touchdown. Place-kicker Joe Perkowski made

Notre Dame's Frank Budka looks surprised as he is pulled down by Dave Meggyesy of Syracuse during the first quarter of the 1961 game.

the extra point and Notre Dame led, 7-0, at the half.

The Irish got their second break when, in the third period, Syracuse fumbled on its own 25. One pass, from Budka to Les Traver, was all Notre Dame needed. With Perkowski again converting, Notre Dame seemed to have a safe 14-0 lead.

The second touchdown, however, must have applied the necessary jolt to the Syracuse offense. Until then, its fine senior quarterback, Dave Sarette, had been unable to complete any of his passes. But he finally got the attack moving. On his own 43-yard line, on a fourth down with one yard to go, he had enough confidence to gamble. He not only went for a first down, but he went for the end zone. Guessing correctly that Notre Dame would be looking for the quarterback sneak, Sarette passed instead to end John Mackey, who outran everyone. Then Sarette gambled again and attempted a two-point conversion; that is, he passed rather than kicked the ball. He was successful and Syracuse trailed, 14-8.

The momentum had suddenly shifted to Syracuse and the Orangemen took advantage early in the fourth quarter. Guiding the team masterfully, Sarette took them down to the Notre Dame seven. He called his own number for a running play, a dangerous play against the inflamed

Notre Dame defense. Sarette picked up four yards, but was hit so hard that he was knocked out. He was carried off the field unconscious. Then sophomore Bob Lelli was sent in to get the toughest three yards of the entire game.

Lelli moved Syracuse to the one, but it was fourth down. Showing the same confidence and daring as Sarette, Lelli rolled out to the right on an option play. Quickly scanning the end zone, he spotted Dick Easterly in the open. Lelli's pass was on target and Syracuse had its second touchdown. This time a two-point conversion was unnecessary. Dick Erickson kicked the extra point and, with just ten minutes left, Syracuse finally had the lead, 15-14.

Then it was Notre Dame's turn to come from behind, and they battled fiercely. Yet it seemed that Syracuse was always poised to make the right move at the crucial moment. Three times Notre Dame had the ball and three times it lost it—once on downs at its own 40, and twice on interceptions. But Syracuse didn't have much better luck at maintaining possession when it was on offense. Twice it had the ball in the last two minutes and couldn't keep it.

With 17 seconds remaining, Notre Dame took possession of the ball for what undoubtedly would be its last chance. And with the ball on its own 30-yard line Notre Dame didn't seem to have much of a chance at all. Budka dropped back to pass and was trapped. Miraculously, he escaped and gained 20 yards. Then he threw to George Sefcik for 11 yards. The clock was stopped and just three seconds were left. Time for only one more play. Even though Perkowski would have to kick from the Syracuse 46, Notre Dame had no choice—it had to attempt a field goal.

A strange silence fell over the crowd as the ball was snapped back to Sefcik, the holder. Perkowski took the kicker's classic steps toward the ball, swung his foot like a pendulum and smashed it against the ball. Everyone's eyes followed the pigskin's flight. Suddenly there was a loud groan. The kick had been wide. Time had run out and it appeared that Notre Dame had gone down to defeat.

But a strange thing was taking place on the field. Those fans who glanced back at Sefcik and Perkowski noticed a red handkerchief near them on the ground. An infraction of the rules had been committed, but by whom? Then the head linesman, F. G. Skibbie, signaled the crime: "roughing the kicker, Syracuse."

Skibbie marched off 15 yards against Syracuse and motioned both teams to the line of scrimmage. Notre Dame was entitled to another play. Naturally the Fighting Irish attempted another field goal. And this time, kicking from the 31,

Joe Perkowski kicks the controversial 31-yard field goal for Notre Dame against Syracuse.

Perkowski made good. The scoreboard flickered for the last time, registering the home team's last three points: Notre Dame 17, Syracuse 15.

A mob of fans rushed onto the field to carry off the Notre Dame players. Another group tried, unsuccessfully, to pull down the steel-based concrete goal posts. No one wanted to go home. The Notre Dame band stayed on the field, playing, long after the game was over.

That night Notre Dame fans celebrated loudly,

while Syracuse fans remained mournfully silent. Meanwhile, someone with a rulebook was doing a little research. And he discovered that the officials had made a fantastic error in permitting Notre Dame to attempt a second kick. The rules specifically stated that the period could not be extended because of a foul on a last-play kick.

Then the arguments began. Syracuse demanded that it be given its rightful victory. Both the Eastern College Athletic Conference and the Big Ten, which had supplied the officials for the game, said they were powerless to change the score. They said that Syracuse could win only if Notre Dame conceded the game.

At that point the issue became a moral one. People all over the country sympathized with Syracuse, saying that Notre Dame officials would never be able to live with themselves if they didn't give back their illegal victory. But Notre Dame refused to do so. They argued that the clock was still running when the infraction occurred; therefore Notre Dame was entitled to a second chance. Photos, however, proved that the clock had stopped just before the interference.

The only clear conclusion to be derived from the bitter argument was that the rule governing the occurrence was far too hazy and needed to be reworded or changed. The following February the collegiate rules committee met and made its decision: In a situation like that of the Syracuse-Notre Dame game, a penalty would be placed on the offending team and another play would be permitted.

Unfortunately, Syracuse couldn't benefit from the ruling they had helped bring about. The loss went into the record books forever. But there was some small consolation. Syracuse still received an invitation to a bowl game. The Liberty Bowl wasn't one of the biggest contests, but the Orangemen were happy nevertheless to beat Miami, 15-14. Notre Dame, on the other hand, was destroyed in its final two games of the season. It lost to Iowa, 42-21, and to Duke, 37-13.

Justice had, in a way, triumphed after all.

19

Rookie from Another World

The rookie stood on the sidelines, his back to his stands, the number on his jersey running down be-between his shoulder blades. The number was 1, but ½ might have been more appropriate. His teammates on the Detroit Lions appeared to be twice his size. He was as thin as a sapling, weighing 155 pounds, standing 5 feet 8 inches tall, and was surrounded by men who towered above him.

He hoped that before the day was over he would be on the field with the Lions, helping them beat the Minnesota Vikings. But he knew that the possibility was unlikely. He was a place-kicker and the Detroit coaches had already announced that another man would kick for this game.

The other man was Wayne Walker, a veteran who, on this afternoon of November 13, 1966, was playing his ninth season in the National Football League. The small man was Garo Yepremian, a rookie who had never seen a football game until October, 1966. In fact, until June, 1966, he had never even seen a *football*.

Garo Yepremian was born on Cyprus, a Mediterranean island where the wheat grows high, the olives are juicy, and sheep and goats abound in rich pastures. He spent his boyhood there and his favorite sport was soccer.

Then, when Garo was 15, his family moved to London. There, he became a salesman in a yard-goods store, and in his spare time he played soccer. He was not an expert in all aspects of that fast, many-faceted game, but he did excel at one thing. He could kick the ball more powerfully and more accurately than anyone on the field.

In June, 1966, Garo came to the United States to visit a brother who had moved to Indianapolis. His brother suggested that he try kicking a football to see how well he could do at that sport. Garo tried, soccer style. He raced up to the ball from the side, swung his left foot into it and connected with the instep instead of the toe—as place-kickers usually do. His style was strange but effective. The ball soared into the air and flew straight and far down the field.

For weeks Garo spent two hours a day kicking

a football. He became so good at it that his brother suggested he try to secure a college football scholarship. Garo agreed and demonstrated his skill for the coach at Butler University. The coach said that there was always a place on his team for a fellow who could kick as well as Garo. However, it was soon discovered that Garo could not be admitted to any college because he did not have a high school diploma.

Undiscouraged, the Yepremian brothers decided to contact some professional teams. They wrote letters to several, asking for a tryout. Some of their friends thought they were being foolish. What pro team would grant a tryout to a 22-year-old who had never even seen a football game?

Then, to everyone's surprise, the Atlanta Falcons decided to give Garo an opportunity to show his skill. So did the Lions. Both tryouts were held in October, and both teams wanted Garo. "I signed with the Lions," he said after making his choice, "because I thought my future here was good."

Indeed, Garo's future did look good when he signed with the Lions. Everything had happened so quickly, as in a dream—the trip to the United States, the introduction to a football, his pride in receiving a Lion uniform, even though the smallest Lion jersey hung all the way down to his knees.

Then, his life began to resemble a nightmare. In his first game, against the Baltimore Colts, he played very poorly. He also played poorly against the Chicago Bears. Many people were saying that the Lions had been foolish to count on Garo's kicking. Sports writers compared him unfavorably with Pete and Charley Gogolak, whose soccer-style kicking had made them stars in professional football. They pointed out that the Gogolak brothers had played football in college and had been in the United States for years before competing against the professional players in the NFL. Garo had been in the United States for only a few months and his performance had fallen far short of expectations.

Now, on November 13, 1966, Garo was in Minnesota, trotting out on the field for pregame practice, although Wayne Walker was going to kick for Detroit that day. He began warming up. His legs felt limber, and strong. He booted football after football between the goal posts. Off to the side, one of the Lions' assistant coaches, Carl Brettschneider, watched with delight. Presently, Brettschneider walked to the sidelines and spoke to head coach Harry Gilmer. "Harry," he said, "Garo is splitting the middle."

"Okay," said Gilmer, "we'll let Garo kick."

Garo sat on the bench and stared as his rival

Garo Yepremian, who had never even seen a football until he came to America in 1966, demonstrates his soccer-style place kicking.

kicker, Minnesota's Fred Cox, booted a 15-yard field goal to put the Vikings ahead, 3-0. He watched as the Vikings scored a touchdown, increasing their lead to 10-0.

Then, in the second quarter, a Lion offensive drive gave him a chance to change the score. He was sent in for the field goal. He raced up to the ball from the side and drove it 33 yards for three points. Minutes later he performed the same feat from the 26-yard line; then again from the 15, and once more from the 20. His four field goals put the Lions ahead at halftime, 12-10.

In the press box, reporters consulted their record books. Garo already had four field goals, and the NFL record for field goals in one game was five. Four men—Ernie Nevers in 1926, Bob Waterfield in 1951, Roger Leclerc in 1961 and Jim Baaken in 1964—shared the record. Now it was threatened by Garo, possibly the most unlikely pro football player the reporters had ever seen.

In the third quarter, Minnesota scored two touchdowns and led, 24-12. Then, Garo resumed his attack on the record. Calmly, confidently, he propelled his instep into the football at the 28-yard line. Instantly, the Lions had three more points. Garo now shared the record with Nevers, Waterfield, Leclerc and Baaken. His teammates hugged him and handed him the ball. "That's yours," one of them said. "For setting the record."

"Wait a minute," another said. "He only tied the record."

They took back the ball, telling Garo he should kick another and really break the record.

Soon Detroit had the ball on the Minnesota 32-yard line, and Garo rushed into the game. Dropping back behind his big linemen, he ran at the ball from the side and swept his instep into it. The ball flew into the air, sped toward the end zone and sailed right between the goal posts. Garo Yepremian, the boy from Cyprus, owned one of the treasured records in American sports.

The Lions drove on and scored two fourth-quarter touchdowns. After each touchdown, Garo kicked the extra point. With one minute, 30 seconds remaining in the game, Detroit was ahead, 32-31. The Vikings took possession of the football for one last try, but it was a futile try. Detroit stopped them and the clock ran out.

As soon as the gun went off, all of the players surged into the locker room, laughing and celebrating the victory. The other players circled Garo, slapping his back and shouting happily.

"I am very excited," he said. "I am very happy about the six goals. I want to inspire my team."

Then Garo, who six months earlier had never seen a football, held aloft the ball he had kicked over the crossbar for his sixth field goal and the National Football League record.

20

Instant Pro Quarterback

Three yards and a cloud of dust. That summed up the kind of football Tom Matte played at Ohio State. His coach had a simple theory about the game—you bang away at the other team's line until it starts buckling. Then you bang away some more.

Matte was Ohio State's quarterback. He was six feet tall, weighed 205 pounds and was a bruising runner and a sharp play caller. Often, under his leadership, Ohio would go through a whole game without putting the ball into the air.

"Once in a while we would put the ball into the air," said Matte. "It was only to show the other guys we could if we had to."

The Baltimore Colts had scouted Matte for three seasons. But they didn't need him as a quarterback. They had Johnny Unitas, the finest passer of the National Football League. When they drafted Matte in 1961, they converted him into a halfback. He became a spot player and was used only when the regular halfback, Lenny Moore, needed a rest.

"Occasionally," said Matte, "I would get in for the option play. I hadn't passed much at college, but I was still a threat to do it. The other side still had to defend against me."

In 1965 Unitas was leading the Colts to the top of the Western Division of the NFL. And his back-up man, Gary Cuozzo, was rapidly developing into a fine quarterback. At the same time, the restless Matte was still sitting on the bench as a reserve halfback.

Then, four games before the end of the season, Unitas suffered a fractured kneecap.

"It's tough losing Unitas. Everybody knows what he means to us," said Coach Don Shula, "but we have Cuozzo. He's a good one. We'll also have Matte work there some just in case . . ."

His voice trailed off. Pro coaches hate to think of losing quarterbacks through injuries. Quarterbacks run the game, set up the offense and often make the difference between winning and losing.

On Sunday, December 12, 1965, the Colts faced Green Bay. A win could assure Baltimore of the division title, but unfortunately Green Bay was ahead. Unitas, dressed in street clothes sat on the sidelines.

When Cuozzo went back to pass, the Packer defense broke through his protection and descended on him. Cuozzo was buried under a pile of emerald-green jerseys. After the players were untangled, he limped off the field with a separated left shoulder.

"Get in there, Tom, and just keep the ball on the ground," Shula told Matte.

"It happened too fast to be afraid. I was calling a play before I knew it," Matte said later.

The college quarterback who had rarely passed was now the offensive leader of a team that was famous for its passing. Matte ran a couple of plays into the line, but Green Bay wouldn't move. Soon Cuozzo reappeared with his shoulder taped, and threw a touchdown pass. But it didn't matter. Green Bay won, 42-27.

After the game, Cuozzo had to be shipped off to the hospital for surgery.

"You're it," said Shula to Matte. "We go as far as you take us."

The Colts played their last game of the season against the Los Angeles Rams. In order to remain in contention they had to win and hope that Green Bay lost or at least tied its last game. In either case, the Colts would meet Green Bay in a play-off game for the division championship.

"I didn't sleep much that week," said Matte. "It's an awful burden running a football team."

Matte worked hard all week in practice. He memorized plays and practiced his formations. He loosened up his long-stilled passing arm.

The Colts obtained Pittsburgh Steeler veteran Ed Brown late in the week to help Matte.

"It's Matte's game," said Shula. "Brown doesn't know our system."

Tom Matte warms his hands while talking with Coach Don Schula (without hat). Matte is wearing a wrist band, on which he has written key plays.

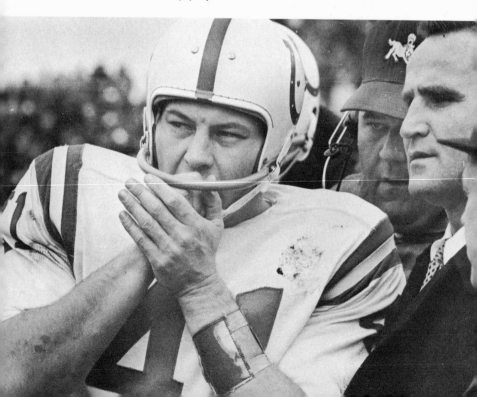

There was one bit of help for the inexperienced quarterback—a roll of tape. Matte put the numbers of a half-dozen running plays on his taped wrists. He had thrown the ball five times all year with only one completion. He wasn't going to win the game in the air.

On most pro teams the quarterback likes to stand and pass. If he gets the right kind of protection he can leave the field with a clean uniform. But on Saturday, December 18, when Matte went out to play, he didn't pass. He ran. He dove into the line and was pounded. He circled his end. He rolled out and ducked past the charging giants of the Rams' line.

Matte led the ground gainers that day with 99 yards in 16 tries. Lou Michaels kicked a field goal and the Colts won, 20-17, as 46,336 Ram fans cheered the courageous performance.

Baltimore now had some hope. Then the next day the unexpected happened—San Francisco tied Green Bay. The Colts, without a real professional quarterback, would now meet the Packers, whose Bart Starr is one of the best quarterbacks in the business.

Fate took a hand early in the play-off game. Starr, trying to make a tackle after a fumble, was knocked cold on the first play of the game. Zeke Bratkowski, Green Bay's number two quarterback and a ten-year veteran, was now matched

Quarterback Matte carries the ball for long yardage during
the all-important game with the Los Angeles Rams in 1965.

with Matte. Bratkowski was a passer in a passing game, while Matte was a runner in a passing game.

The Colts' defense was splendid, and Matte ran the offense conservatively. With one minute and 58 seconds left, the Colts led, 10-7. Don Shinnick had recovered a fumble for a touchdown and Michaels had kicked a field goal.

Then the Packers' Don Chandler, bald and aging, trotted onto the frozen field at Green Bay to try for the tying points. The clock showed Baltimore only 118 seconds away from one of football's biggest upsets.

Chandler kicked the football. It went up, swerved toward the right and flopped into the stands. Chandler stared for an instant and shook his head. He thought it had missed. Most of the hometown crowd gasped. They agreed with Chandler.

Referee Jim Tunney had stared at the ball closely for a long instant and finally shot his hands into the air. Green Bay had tied the score, 10-10, on Chandler's field goal.

"It was at an angle," Chandler said later. "It was hard to tell if it was good. I was shaking my head because it didn't split the uprights. It might have missed and we would have lost right there."

The game went into sudden-death overtime, tied at 10-10. For 13 minutes and 39 seconds the

Colts held firm. Then Green Bay reached the Colts' 22-yard line. Chandler came in again.

Matte stood on the sideline, a brave but helpless figure. He had done all he could do. Chandler kicked. The ball split the uprights perfectly and Green Bay won the play-off, 13-10. Matte, the substitute quarterback, had failed.

The winning score had been a 22-yard field goal, perhaps the easiest scoring play in football.

"At least," said Matte, who had come so close to a well-deserved triumph, "they didn't beat us on a pass."

21

Roses Bloom in the Snow

In 1950, as the Big Ten football season entered its final week, it looked as if there would be a new champion. Although Michigan had dominated the league during the previous three years, with two outright titles and a tie, the Wolverines were not considered the top contender in 1950. In fact, they needed a double miracle if they expected to win an unprecedented fourth straight championship.

First, Illinois (with a conference record of four wins and one loss) would have to lose to Northwestern (two wins and three losses). And then Michigan (three wins, one loss and one tie) would have to beat Ohio State (five wins and one loss). Both possibilities seemed absurd—especially that of Michigan beating Ohio State.

The Wolverines also had two nonconference losses on their record—to Michigan State (which was not yet considered a Big Ten member in football) and to Army. If by chance the Michigan team should win the Big Ten title again and therefore earn the right to play in the Rose Bowl, its 5-3-1 overall record would be the worst of any Rose Bowl team since 1916.

Because of this unimpressive record Big Ten officials, who were concerned about the conference's image, weren't pulling too hard for a Michigan miracle. They considered Ohio State or Illinois to be a far more impressive representative.

Michigan, of course, had no control over the outcome of the Illinois-Northwestern game, and many people felt that the Wolverines would have as little control in their own game. That season Ohio State's fearsome offensive machine had scored 83 points against an Iowa team that had given up no more than 21 points to anyone else. Ohio State had also beaten Minnesota, 48-0. But when Michigan played Minnesota, the Wolverines were considered fortunate to come off the field with a 7-7 tie.

In addition to the championship's being at stake, there was the drama of having Ohio State's defensive guard Bob Momsen pitted against his brother, linebacker Tony Momsen of Michigan. There was also the attraction of two great offensive stars—Vic Janowicz, Ohio State's tailback, and Chuck Ortmann, Michigan's tailback. Janowicz was a unanimous All-America choice, and overshadowed the Michigan tailback. But Ortmann was just as valuable to Michigan as Janowicz was to Ohio. Both men ran, passed and punted and the forthcoming game hinged largely on whose triple-threat skills were superior that day.

Adding to the drama was the pressure on Ohio State's coach, Wes Fesler. He was the team's fifth coach in the past decade, and Ohio State was beginning to acquire a reputation as a "coach's graveyard." The school's alumni and the home-town boosters in Columbus were probably the most outspoken in the country. Often they were not even satisfied with winning a game. For example, after State's 48-0 victory over Minnesota, an Ohio fan confronted Fesler and accused him of holding down the score. With such avid rooters criticizing his strategy, it was not surprising that Fesler felt his job might be in jeopardy if he didn't beat Michigan.

Actually, no one—not even the most eager Michigan supporter—envisioned an upset. In fact, Michigan athletic director Fritz Crisler admitted after the game that he hadn't bothered to send a man to scout California (bound for the Rose Bowl) in their game against Stanford; he thought the effort would be "a waste of time."

Despite the expectation of a lopsided contest, the 78,726 seats in Ohio Stadium had been sold long before the game. Ohio State and Michigan had been traditional rivals for decades, and even a meaningless game between them was sure to be a sellout.

A couple of days before the game, the weather bureau reported that a violent blizzard was moving down from the north. It was expected to reach the Ohio area just in time for the kickoff. But the storm hit even sooner. The roads were covered with ice, and a 28-mile-per-hour wind buffeted the snow into a swirling frenzy. The arctic conditions were the worst to hit the Midwest in years and rumors spread that the game would be canceled.

On Saturday morning, November 25, radio broadcasters in and around Columbus were announcing every few minutes that the game would still be played. A third of the people with tickets were unable to attend the game. Fifty thousand, though, were on hand for the opening kickoff, looking down on a white field whose yard markers had been obliterated. The temperature was ten degrees above zero.

It was obvious from the outset that standard football strategy would be useless. The fierce weather conditions would neutralize both teams

It was obvious from the outset of the 1950 Michigan-Ohio
State game that standard football strategy would be useless.

and one lucky play might mean the difference between victory and defeat. Caution was the important thing; each team had to bide its time, hoping the other would make a mistake.

Ohio State kicked off, and for the first few minutes the game was almost comical. Rather than risk a run or a pass deep in Michigan territory, Ortmann punted on first down. Ohio State ran a play, but got nowhere. Then Janowicz quick-kicked and the ball soared 57 yards to the Michigan six. Again the Wolverines punted on first down. This time, however, Bob Monsen crashed through the Michigan line to block the kick. Ohio took possession of the ball and set up a 38-yard field-goal attempt by Janowicz. Officials strained to spot the ball as it sailed through the blinding snowflakes. The kick was good and Ohio State led, 3-0. But before the first quarter ended Michigan had picked up two points on a safety by blocking a punt in the Ohio State end zone.

It had become apparent that punting or quick-kicking could be just as dangerous as trying to run or throw the ball. The danger was even more pointedly emphasized late in the first half. Ohio State, nursing a 3-2 lead, had a third down with six yards to go for a first down around their own 14-yard line (there was too much snow to determine the exact spot). Forty-seven seconds

were left and Michigan called time out. The
Wolverines, trying to outguess their opponent,
thought that State might quick-kick once again.
So they arranged to shift two men over to the left
side to try to break in and block the kick. They
guessed that State would be using only one
blocker to protect the kicker. As a result, one of
the two defenders might get through.

Michigan's strategy would work only if State
did indeed decide to kick. But there were many
Ohio rooters and sports writers who believed that
a kick would be foolish. Why risk a blocked kick,
they reasoned, when two rushing plays would
probably use up the remaining time in the half.
But Coach Fesler was concerned about the possibility of a fumble. So he sent in halfback Bob
Demmel with orders for Janowicz to punt on the
next play.

Janowicz dropped back inside his own five-
yard line. The ball was snapped. Two Wolverines
crashed over the left side. One went for the
blocker. The other, Tony Momsen, went for the
punter. Tony blocked the kick and the ball skid-
ded into the end zone. Momsen quickly spotted
the ball. Scrambling after it, he dove on it for a
Michigan touchdown. The extra point was good
and the Wolverines led at the half, 9-3.

The second half amounted to a waste of time.
Neither team produced even the semblance of a

Michigan's Chuck Ortmann kicks from behind his own goal line during the first quarter of the "Snow Bowl."

scoring threat. As Michigan coach Bernie Osterbaan said later, "It was such a horrible day that
we tried to get rid of the ball and let the other fellow make the mistakes."

Ohio State, although trailing, hoped for a Michigan mistake, too. Punt after punt slid off the toes
of Ortmann and Janowicz. By the time the game
ended, with the score still 9-3, Janowicz had
punted 24 times, Ortmann 21. Their combined
total of 45 was an all-time record.

As the frozen fans scurried out of the stadium,
they could not decide whether they had seen the
season's most exciting game or its dullest. But the
Ohio rooters, who, of course, were unhappy with
the 9-3 Michigan victory, agreed that they had
seen the luckiest team of all time. Michigan had
made no first downs, completed no passes and
gained just 27 yards rushing.

After the game, Coach Osterbaan, aware that
Fesler might take unnecessary blame for the defeat, tried to soften the situation with logic and
sympathy. "Imagine having a great team like
Fesler has," said Osterbaan, "and not being able
to use it because of the weather conditions."

While Osterbaan talked to reporters, the Michigan players dressed slowly, waiting for word of
the Illinois-Northwestern game, which wasn't
over yet. It seemed an eternity for the numb
Wolverines. At last the game ended: Northwest-

ern 14, Illinois 7. The steamy dressing room suddenly became a bedlam of delirious Michigan players. Illinois' defeat meant that the Wolverines would play California in the Rose Bowl. As someone later described Michigan's good fortune: Roses had bloomed in the snow.

Two other items complete the incredible story of what has gone down in history as the "Snow Bowl." Two weeks later, Fesler became fed up with all the harsh criticism of his coaching and resigned from Ohio State. He did not remain inactive for long, however. A couple of months later he accepted the job as head coach at Minnesota.

The second item concerns the outcome of the Rose Bowl game. Big Ten officials needn't have worried about the ability of the Wolverines to uphold the league's prestige. California took an undefeated record into the 1951 New Year's Day game, but after the final whistle had blown, it too, like Ohio State, was wondering what black magic Michigan possessed. Final score: Michigan 14, California 6.

22

The Biggest Blunder

The cold, driving rain failed to dampen the spirits of the Dartmouth undergraduates. Several hundred had braved the weather on that Friday night of November 15, 1940, and gathered at the north end of the campus. Many were attempting to warm themselves around a pathetically small fire.

Lou Young, the captain of the Dartmouth football team, stood on a wooden box and addressed the crowd.

"We're not going out there to lose," he said. "You're going to see a fighting Dartmouth team tomorrow."

The crowd applauded Young. They knew that the Indians had done their best to be ready for the game, but they still could not avoid being slightly intimidated by their opponents.

Dartmouth, loser of four games that season, would meet Cornell as a decided underdog. The Big Red of Cornell had not lost a game in three seasons. They were coming into the Dartmouth game with an undefeated, untied record for the 1940 season.

"Cornell's only problem is overconfidence," one sports writer wrote. "They may be looking ahead to the Penn game."

Pennsylvania had tied Cornell, 0-0, in 1938. It was the only blemish on Cornell's record in three seasons.

By Saturday afternoon the weather hadn't improved much. When the game began, the spectators were already shivering in their seats. Dartmouth, coached by Earl Blaik, surprised Cornell almost from the opening kickoff. The Indians tackled hard on defense and blocked hard on offense. Cornell, coached by Carl Snavely, was heavier, more experienced, quicker. Yet they couldn't move the ball.

At halftime there was still no score. Blaik, talking to his team in the locker room, said:

"One score might win it. Let's go out there and get it."

Early in the fourth quarter, with the game still scoreless, Bob Krieger kicked a 27-yard field

Referee Red Friesell watches Cornell punt during the disputed 1940 game with Dartmouth.

goal for the Indians, buoying up Dartmouth's hopes.

"We've got to hold them now," said Blaik.

Cornell fought back bravely. But the Indians held. Now the clock was on Dartmouth's side.

A forward pass gave Cornell a first down on the Dartmouth six-yard line. Only 45 seconds remained in the game as the Big Red lined up for the play.

Mort Lansberg, the big Cornell fullback slashed to the three. Walt Scholl, the tailback, was given the ball and drove to the one-yard line. Lansberg then spun into the line and was stopped a foot short of the goal.

Now only nine seconds remained. At this point Snavely called a time-out to stop the clock.

Referee Red Friesell blew his whistle to announce a penalty and called for the ball.

"Delay of the game against Cornell," he told the Dartmouth captain.

Friesell stepped off the five yards and gave the ball to Cornell. Scholl took the snap from center, faded back and aimed a pass at a receiver in the end zone. Ray Hall, the Dartmouth fullback, leaped high and knocked the ball down at the goal line.

The game was all over for Cornell, it seemed. The crowd cheered and Dartmouth moved to take over the ball. But there was confusion on the field. Friesell was not sure if the last play had occurred on the third or fourth down. He did not know which team should have possession of the ball. He started to turn the ball over to Dartmouth, but stopped. Linesman Joe McKenny held up his hand.

"Cornell ball," said McKenny, "fourth down coming up."

Friesell, confused by the penalty, had lost count of the downs. He gave the ball to Cornell again.

With the clock reading three seconds, Scholl

passed into the end zone and end Bill Murphy caught it for a touchdown. Then after the gun had sounded, Cornell kicked the extra point and apparently won, 7-3.

Friesell ran off the field and into the referee's quarters. Later, as he stood under the shower, Howie Odell, scouting for Penn, rushed into the room.

"Five downs," he said, "Cornell had five downs, Red. All the fellows in the press box agree with me."

"If that's true," said Friesell, "I'll try to reverse the score."

The possibility that the touchdown play had been illegal was pointed out to Cornell's president, Edmund E. Day, and the athletic director, Jim Lynah.

Later that evening they sent a wire to Dartmouth officials:

IF THE OFFICIALS IN CHARGE OF TODAY'S GAME RULE AFTER INVESTIGATION THAT THERE WERE FIVE DOWNS IN THE FINAL SERIES AND THE WINNING TOUCHDOWN WAS MADE ON AN ILLEGAL FIFTH DOWN, THE SCORE WILL BE RECORDED AS A 3-0 DARTMOUTH WIN.

Both Cornell and Dartmouth had taken game films. The films were hastily developed and were ready for showing late the next evening, and Friesell viewed them in the Dartmouth athletic office.

"I saw the sequence of plays," he said, "and I was wrong. I gave Cornell an illegal extra down. It was totally my fault."

Cornell had indeed scored on an illegal, extra fifth down. Friesell immediately contacted Commissioner Asa Bushnell of the Eastern Collegiate Football Association and advised him of the error. But Bushnell pointed out that once a game is over the officials have no authority to change the score.

The problem was complicated. Friesell, one of the finest referees in the country, had publicly admitted that he had been wrong. But the game had been entered in the record books. And the error was part of the game.

Cornell's Coach Snavely concluded that the only honorable solution was to concede the game to Dartmouth. Snavely sent a wire to Blaik. The president of Cornell sent an identical wire to the president of Dartmouth:

WE CONGRATULATE YOU ON THE VICTORY OF YOUR FINE TEAM. THE CORNELL TOUCHDOWN WAS SCORED ON A FIFTH DOWN AND WE RE-LINQUISH CLAIM TO THE VICTORY AND EXTEND CONGRATULATIONS TO DARTMOUTH.

The news touched off a snake dance by Dartmouth students. They cheered their team at a rally and Captain Young was hoisted in the air by excited students. Cornell's winning streak was over. Dartmouth had achieved a great upset.

The record books now show that Dartmouth won that day, 3-0, but the honesty of Red Friesell and the sportsmanship of Cornell will always make the "fifth down" game an afternoon to remember.

23

Medical Miracle

Since joining the Green Bay Packers in 1958, Jerry Kramer has developed into one of the finest offensive guards in the NFL. There are many reasons for his success. One is his size. He stands 6 feet 3 inches and weighs 260 pounds. Another is his ability to hold his ground to protect the passer or to shove his opponent aside on a drive through the line. He also has speed.

Over the years the Packers have become known for their power sweep around end. This type of running play relies on blocking by two or more linemen. The play is doomed, however, if Kramer and his running mate, Fuzzy Thurston, are unable to move to the side fast enough to open a path around end for the ball carrier. The play has been successful more often than not because

Jerry Kramer (64) and teammate open up a perfect hole for running back Jim Taylor.

Kramer has bulldozed his way through would-be tacklers.

But Kramer's assets would not be worth very much if he did not have an abundance of one thing—courage. "Nothing intimidates Kramer," Packer coach Vince Lombardi once wrote. "If you told him to throw a block on a trailer, he'd give it a try. . . . He ignores not only the small hurts but the large ones, too. The evidence of his indifference is all over his body."

To survive pro football a player must be able to ignore pain. No one in the history of the game has had better preparation in this respect than Kramer. Beginning at the age of five Jerry was the victim of a series of bizarre and agonizing accidents. The story of his youth in Sandpoint, Idaho, resembles a tale of horror, but every word is true.

One day his older brother had left an axe lying in the yard, so Jerry decided to help his mother by cutting some firewood. The huge axe probably weighed more than Jerry, but somehow he managed to get it over his head. Holding it up became a problem and Jerry's arms buckled under the weight. The axe slipped and, as it fell, sliced Jerry's chin. The cut was serious and it produced a cleft that is still visible today.

Jerry's next accident occurred when he was a high-school sophomore. While in the school's woodworking shop, he backed into an electric lathe. The machine severely lacerated his side. He was rushed to the doctor but, surprisingly, Jerry was more concerned about missing that night's football game than he was about his wound. After stitching Jerry's side, the doctor gave him permission to kick off, but told him not to make tackles. That night Jerry kicked off. Then, without thinking, he charged downfield to help make the tackle. In doing so, he tore loose all of his stitches and had to leave the game.

Then one day in the fall of 1952, when he was 17, Jerry was hunting in the woods. After walking a good distance, he sat down on a rock to rest. He placed his grandfather's old double-barreled shotgun against the rock and cocked it so it would be ready if he saw any game. Suddenly there was a terrible explosion. The shotgun had slipped from the rock. Both barrels had gone off and their loads had smashed into Jerry's right forearm and side.

In the hospital, the doctor discovered that the blast had mutilated the inside of Jerry's forearm. Several doctors were brought in for consultation. Many years later Jerry would still remember the chill he had felt when one of the doctors touched his bandaged arm with the end of a pencil to indicate the spot where the arm might have to be amputated. His arm was finally saved—after a series of operations and many blood transfusions

—but he would always bear a large scar. In addition, the fingers of his right hand would be half clenched for the rest of his life.

The following summer Jerry had another mishap; it turned out to be the worst accident of his life. He was chasing a calf in the yard and finally cornered it near a woodpile. The frightened calf brought its hoof down on a wooden plank, splintering it. The jagged end of the plank shot up, penetrating Jerry's groin like a spear. He didn't find out until later how lucky he was. The shaft had missed severing the body's main artery by just a quarter-inch.

Some splinters were removed from the wound, but Jerry didn't recover normally. Three weeks later he was taken to Spokane, Washington, where doctors subjected him to a long and painful examination. Finally they found the problem. A sliver of wood seven inches long and three-quarters of an inch thick had worked its way up into a muscle and was within a half-inch of penetrating Jerry's back. They operated and removed the splinter.

In spite of his gruesome medical history, Jerry went on to stardom as a lineman at the University of Idaho. But he wasn't without medical problems there, either. He chipped a vertebra in his neck and had to have another operation. The surgery left an ugly scar on his neck and it was visible through his crew cut, too. In the years to come the scar would inspire his Packer teammates to affectionately call him "Zipperhead,"—that is, when they weren't calling him "The Claw" in honor of his mangled right hand.

Jerry was such an outstanding lineman while at the University of Idaho that the Packers drafted him as their Number Four choice after the 1957 season. It was a wise choice and the Packers and Jerry Kramer achieved fame together. In Jerry's rookie year, the Packers won only one game. Two years later they had won the Western Conference title and Kramer was selected an All-Pro lineman.

But the Packers lost the championship play-off to Philadelphia, 17-13. During the game Kramer played with only ten-percent vision in his left eye. He had suffered a detached retina during an earlier game, but wouldn't submit to surgery until after the end of the season.

In 1961 Jerry broke his ankle, which, to him, was certainly nothing to get upset about, although some people insisted he would never again play pro football. But in 1962 Jerry was back in the starting lineup and played a big role in the Packers' successful drive for the NFL championship. That season he made nine field goals in 11 attempts and 39 extra points out of 40.

Then in 1963 Kramer began to have difficulty

maintaining his playing weight. By the end of the season he had dropped to 237 pounds. Obviously something was wrong. But the problem didn't sideline Kramer until the second game of 1964 when, weak and feverish, Jerry asked to be taken out of the game.

Within the next five days Jerry had to undergo two operations. Doctors thought there was a 95-percent chance that he had cancer. They soon found a growth about the size of a grapefruit near Kramer's diaphragm. One doctor described the growth as "a woody, hard thing." Laboratory tests, however, revealed that it was non-malignant. The immediate problem was to treat the massive infection.

After leaving the hospital Kramer tried to rejoin the team, which had lost two games by a one-point margin during his absence. But he still had a hole in his chest, in which doctors packed fresh gauze each day. But the hole wouldn't drain properly. He was dropped from the Packer roster in early November and sent to the famed Mayo Clinic in Rochester, Minnesota. There, doctors discovered that he now had a hole in his intestines.

After more surgery he returned to Green Bay, weighing just 210 pounds. Many people thought that Kramer was dying. In fact, right after Christmas a rumor of his death began to circulate and some friends called his home to express their sorrow.

For the next few months Jerry tried to live his normally active life. He hunted alligators with bow and arrow in the swamps of Louisiana and went scuba diving in the Gulf of Mexico. In fact, his doctors had difficulty preventing him from going to the Arctic Circle to hunt grizzly bears. But they were relieved that he felt well enough to be so active. The wound in his chest, however, continued to drain; it needed further attention. Kramer went back to the Mayo Clinic, but the cause of the persistent infection could not be found.

Afterward he went to his own doctor in Green Bay, who suggested another exploratory operation. Kramer was on the operation table for six and a half hours and required four transfusions. But the doctor was determined to find out why new holes had developed in Kramer's large and small intestines. Finally, he discovered a four-inch sliver of wood, about the size of a ballpoint pen, and two smaller splinters. They had been puncturing holes in Kramer's intestines and were, of course, the remaining pieces of the plank that had penetrated his groin 12 years earlier.

Kramer felt his health problems were over, and he wanted to return to the Packers. Perhaps to keep him from building up false hopes, Coach

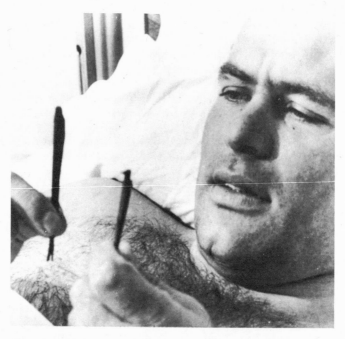

Kramer holds up two of the three splinters of wood that were removed from his body during surgery. They resulted from a boyhood accident that had occurred 12 years before.

Vince Lombardi wasn't very encouraging. When Jerry told him he intended to play, Lombardi said, "That's wonderful, but I don't think you're going to make it."

If Lombardi really believed what he was telling Kramer, he was wrong. For after a gingerly start during the 1965 season, Jerry gradually picked up momentum. Eventually he was at least as good as he had been before.

Coincidentally or not, Jerry's return to form

was accompanied by a return to championship glory for the Packers. Green Bay won the NFL title in 1965 and the following season won the historic first Super Bowl game, against the AFL champion Kansas City Chiefs. During the big victories, Kramer was leading the Packers' power sweeps just as he had done before.

Even if Jerry Kramer had never become a great offensive guard, the fact that he has been able to play the game at all would make him football's medical miracle.

Index

Page numbers in italics refer to photographs